MUSIC THERAPY

IN

PALLIATIVE/HOSPICE CARE

by

SUSAN MUNRO

LGSM(MT), MTA, CMT

Cover design by Fredi Jaggi, DESIGNLINK, MONTREAL/Canada

MMB

MAGNAMUSIC-BATON, INC.

MUSIC THERAPY IN PALLIATIVE/HOSPICE CARE

Susan Munro, LGSM(MT) MTA, CMT

Music Therapy in Palliative/Hospice Care
Gustav Fischer Verlag Stuttgart/New York
English version published by Magnamusic-Baton, Inc., 10370 Page Industrial Boulevard, St. Louis, MO 63132, USA

ISBN 0-918812-37-2

CONTENTS

PART ONE

HOME CARE

CONSULTATION

PALLIATIVE CARE INPATIENT UNIT

PART TWO

TO HEIDI AND TONY

ACKNOWLEDGEMENTS

ARNO PRESS — for quotations from I. Ajemian's and B. Mount's *THE RVH MANUAL ON PALLIATIVE/HOSPICE CARE.* (Ajemian, I. and Mount, B. ed.) New York, Arno Press, 1980.

AMERICAN JOURNAL OF NURSING COMPANY - for a quotation from the American Journal of Nursing, February, 1970.

HARPER AND ROW, PUBLISHER INC. - for a quotation from P. Aries' DEATH INSIDE OUT in *DEATH INSIDE OUT.* The Hastings Center Report. (Steinfels, P. and Veatch, M. ed.) New York, Harper and Row, 1974.

RIDGEVIEW PUBLISHING COMPANY - for a quotation from C. Kenny's *THE MYTHIC ARTERY,* The Magic of Music Therapy. Atascadera, CA 93433, Ridgeview Publishing Company, 1982.

BEACON PRESS - for a quotation from V. Frankl's *MAN'S SEARCH FOR MEANING.* Boston, Beacon Press, 1963.

PREFACE

The challenge of developing a health care service at the Royal Victoria Hospital to meet the needs of dying patients and their families was formidable. It was soon discovered that traditional medical tools were inadequate to treat even the physical symptoms of advanced disease, yet these patients confronted us as well with a host of other problems. The pain of fear, anxiety, emotional isolation; the despair in the face of relentless disease; the concern for family members faced with impending loss; the search for philosophical answers to put suffering in some context of meaning -- how to begin to be helpful in these areas? The inadequacy of the traditional medical orientation led to the search for answers in other disciplines and the development of a multidisciplinary palliative care team.

When Susan Munro joined us as the music therapist on our multidisciplinary Palliative/Hospice Care Team, I soon learned how little I understood of the potential of music. As a physician I had always enjoyed music; as a celebration of life, as a social event, in the many quiet personal moments. Yet I had never attempted to integrate music in my professional work. Now I saw patients sharing a common heritage drawn together by shared music into a supportive community. I saw taut faces and rigid muscles relax before the strains of calm, reassuring rhythms. I witnessed patients whose emotions were locked behind controlled exteriors, able to communicate something of their inner being through the symbolism of music. I observed music facilitating the review of a lifetime of memories, affirming that life had had value, bridging the past to the present, and the present to the future for those who would be left behind. No medication or other treatment technique approached the diversity in potential.

Although it quickly became apparent that music offered an important dimension in our search for ways to meet complex needs, success did not come easily. Traditional medical teams need to learn how to integrate non-medical members, and role redefinition can be slow and difficult. Each patient presents a unique constellation of symptoms, attitudes and values, and any approach must be individual. That which is highly beneficial to one patient or family may be inappropriate or intrusive to the next. The team must learn how to be comfortable with uncertainty and extreme flexibility.

This book presents some of the successes, questions and problems encountered in our attempt to incorporate music therapy in our treatment armamentarium. Reflected as well are Susan's commitment to the patient, her personal honesty and rejection of facile answers, her openness and willingness to share her perspective as a music therapist in the context of the multidisciplinary team. The book should be required reading for all those who work with the terminally ill and seek a new therapeutic approach.

Ina Ajemian, M.D., C.C.F.P.
Assistant Director
Palliative Care Service

INTRODUCTION

A couple of years ago, when I was first asked to write a handbook on the subject of music therapy in palliative care, I simply refused. I considered my experience and knowledge in this field inadequate and too limited to warrant documentation. For every fragment of understanding and insight I gradually gained in this work, many more questions, uncertainties and concerns surfaced. Today I have a few more answers yet still many uncertitudes and queries. In finally accepting the challenge to share my experiences and thoughts on the subject I respond to a demonstrated interest and curiosity about this topic and intend to draw attention to the unique scope of music therapy in the care of dying persons.

I feel very privileged to have shared in the endeavours of the Royal Victoria Hospital's Palliative Care Service. While this involvement stretched my personal make-up and framework as well as my professional skills to challenging limits, it offered at the same time unlimited opportunites for personal and professional exploration and growth. I now understand that music therapy has a significant contribution to make in terminal care and sense a readiness within the palliative/hospice care movement to consider music therapy as a viable adjunct therapy.

In general, hospice care professionals know little about music therapy and music therapists are unfamiliar with terminal care. This manual attempts to bridge the gap. It was commissioned by the German Association for Music Therapy and Gustav Fischer Press as part of a series of handbooks published for music therapists. In choosing the present format I hoped as well to reach other health care professionals involved in palliative care and thus broaden their understanding of the possibilities music therapy offers in this field.

These accounts are written from the perspective of a particular setting, A Palliative Care Service within a University teaching hospital. The reader is asked to perceive them in this context. (see: Royal Victoria Hospital, Palliative Care Service: A brief overview, p. viii). Hospice programs vary greatly in their structure and therefore require adaptation of various music therapy approaches. The structure of the Royal Victoria Hospital's Palliative Care Service afforded me the opportunity of working simultaneously throughout the general hospital, in home care and in an inpatient terminal care ward. The reader can deduce different approaches and considerations of music's therapeutic potential from the various case studies.

I am indebted to many individuals who have knowingly and unknowingly contributed to the writing and content of this book; to Volker Bolay and Gustav Fischer Press for their persuasive insistence in convincing me to accept the challenge of writing these pages; to Fredi Jaggi who captured symbols of movement, vibration, continuity, holism and man in the cover design; to Dr. Balfour Mount for taking the risk of hiring me as the first music therapist in the Palliative Care Service; to Dr. Ina Ajemian, Dr. Edward Furcha and Darlene Berringer for invaluable editorial advise and assistance; to Dr. Marcel Boisvert and Lise Laberge for their personal narratives; to my many colleagues and friends of the PCS for their precious support and good humour in helping me deal with my "staff stress"; to

Carolyn Kenny for her kindred spirit and spark of magic; and to my music therapy friends in Canada and around the world for sharing with me their search for new threads in the fabric of music therapy.

I could not have developed nor formulated the concepts in this manual if it were not for the many patients who shared their "music person" as well as their thoughts and feelings in the face of struggles with terminal illness.

Their gift and insight continues to live on through the pages of this book, and I am particularly grateful to the families who gave permission for inclusion of the pictures.

SUSAN MUNRO

PALLIATIVE/HOSPICE CARE: a definition

palliative care — the primary dictionary meaning of the term "to palliate" is "to reduce the violence of; abate". In the Hospice context, (the care of the terminally ill patient) it means the reduction or abatement of pain and other troubling symptoms by appropriate coordination of all elements of care needed to achieve relief from distress. This term can be considered synonymous with "Hospice Care". (1)

THE PALLIATIVE CARE SERVICE: ROYAL VICTORIA HOSPITAL, MONTREAL

A BRIEF OVERVIEW

This service was instituted at the Royal Victoria Hospital (an eight-hundred and fifty bed teaching hospital affiliated with McGill University) in January 1975, in an attempt to better meet the total needs (physical, psychological, social and spiritual) of terminally ill patients and their families. The Palliative Care Service (PCS) comprises five clinical arms:

1. THE PALLIATIVE CARE INPATIENT UNIT (PCU)

Patients on this eighteen-bed ward have been followed by physicians of the Royal Victoria Hospital. Priority is given to:

a) patients requiring admission from the home care program

b) hospitalized patients difficult to manage in other departments because of poorly controled physical symptoms or difficult psychosocial problems.

Concern for the well-being of the family is considered an acceptable indication for admission of a patient to the PCU. It has been observed that a brief "respite admission" of several days ("to give the family a rest") frequently pays rich dividends in renewed physical and emotional resources for those giving home care, thus enabling a greater number of families to care for their loved ones at home until the end. (2)

Patients on the PCU are cared for by a multidisciplinary team of nurses, doctors, volunteers, chaplain, social worker, physio/occupational therapist and music therapist. At the present time, the average length of patient stay on the PCU is 23.81 days, the median stay 10.0 days. (3)

2. THE HOME CARE SERVICE

This consists of a team of four full-time nurses, with back up from the PCS physician and other palliative care support staff (chaplain, music therapist, occupational/physiotherapist, volunteers). Patients are referred to the home care program

a) when further therapy, aimed at modifying the natural history of the disease, is inappropriate in the opinion of the referring physician.

b) when they are still receiving active therapy with a view to the control of disease, but prognosis is very poor.

The PCS home care service draws patients from approximately half of the island of Montreal, resulting in travel time between patient's homes of 45 minutes or less. (4)

3. THE CONSULTATION SERVICE

The consultation service functions as a symptom control team which sees patients in all departments of the general hospital. It plays a central role in coordinating the continuum of care for terminally ill patients, i.e. hospital community ⟷ home care ⟷ palliative care unit.

The team (consulting a physician), a nurse consultant, an assistant nurse, resource staff of the Palliative Care Service (chaplain, music therapist and a small team of volunteers) work in close collaboration with the personnel of the various departments where patients are hospitalized. Thus, staff throughout the hospital is encouraged to develop palliative care skills and attitudes.

Requests for involvement of the consultation team may be to

- advise in symptom control
- identify psychosocial needs of patient and/or family, and coordinate resources towards meeting these needs
- identify staff problem(s) in handling a particular patient and use PCS resources to supplement those of the primary team
- assess for transfer to the Palliative Care Unit
- coordinate discharge planning, either to the PCS Home Care Service or other community resources
- be of assistance because the patient is dying even when no specific problem is identified. (5)

4. PALLIATIVE CARE CLINIC

The PCS has recently added a fifth clinical arm in the form of a palliative care clinic for the follow up of outpatients and their families. Patients include those from the PCS Home Care program and other Royal Victoria Hospital patients with advanced disease. The initial visits to the PCS clinic may be held while patients are still being followed in the active treatment oncology clinics. This facilitates the transition from life-prolonging to palliative intervention by building a supporting network of relations with those whose expertise will be increasingly relevant to the patient and family as health deteriorates.

A team of trained volunteers, the social worker, physiotherapist, chaplain, music therapist as well as Consultation and Home Care nurses complement the efforts of the PCS clinic physician and nurses as required. Once again the focus is on whole person health care, considering the patient in the context of his family. (6)

5. BEREAVEMENT FOLLOW-UP SERVICE

The goal of this program is to provide support during the initial period of bereavement by offering the opportunity to review the experience with a staff member. The kinds of issues with which many families are concerned are relationships, the diagnosis, cause of treatment, the medical institutions or their role as care givers and the death event itself. Present and anticipated situations in relation to family life, moving, job or child care are often reviewed as well. Information is offered on community resources, including local medical clinics, social service agencies, peer groups or classes. (7)

Such support helps the recently bereaved to cope better with the various difficulties and transitions in grieving and to readjust to continued living after the loss of a loved one. Unusual or exaggerated difficulties in grieving might be observed and referral to professional help can be made.

Research data suggests that such preventative intervention with the bereaved is beneficial in promoting normal recovery from grief and reduces extreme psychological and physical stress which might lead to health and emotional problems. (8)

PART ONE

HOME CARE

CASE 1

NOTE AND OBSERVE

- individual was an exceptional person and patient
- evolution of music experience
- repercussion of music therapy on family
- the memories of the widow

Gérard died of cancer of the kidneys on February 7, 1981, aged 49. For 5 months prior to his death, he had been followed by the PCS Home Care Service. The home care nurse asked me to see him after she had made a few initial visits because she sensed that the arts were an important part of his life. By this time he was quite housebound. He had adjusted to doing some work for the office when he felt well enough and to pursuing some of his hobbies at other times. In a conservatory-like corner of the living room stood an easel and some finished and some unfinished paintings (landscapes, still-lifes). The stereo set looked well-used, some records leaning casually against the shelf rather than being neatly filed away.

He was curious about my profession so we talked briefly about the subject of music therapy, gradually focusing more directly on music, its role in society, history and the life of individuals. Where did it fit into Gérard's life? He was French Canadian. There had been singing with his family and friends, some piano playing years ago, some friends who were musicians. Now, in his illness there was time to indulge in music listening in a way he hadn't previously had time for. He loved it. "Sometimes I've thought of buying a piano. Who knows, maybe when our little girl is a bit older."

I mentioned I could bring him an autoharp; it was easy to play, he could sing to it, he could share with his daughter. He was enthusiastic about the idea.

My next visit centered around the autoharp. From his comments I had observed that he was a "self starter". I gave him few instructions, let him explore and ask questions. We sang a round of "Frère Jacques" (one chord) and "Ah, si mon moine voulait bien danser" (two chords). He quickly picked up the idea of chording and I encouraged him to trust his very musical ear, rather than get stuck in instruction books. Christmas wasn't far off, so I left him with a small carol book.

The autoharp took its place in Gérard's activities but it wasn't long before his focus turned to the question of a piano. Where could one buy one in the city? What kind? How much should one spend? He differed greatly from the majority of patients I saw. There never was a mention of "What for? It's not worth it. I don't have long anyway". He saw healing and renewing potential in music making. My visits had possibly helped to bring these perceptions into the foreground, but their seeds lay within Gérard's personality and life view.

Since I first met him, he had become weaker. Large amounts of fluid were frequently drained from his abdomen, yet he and his wife Lise went out to buy a piano, visiting three stores to find what they wanted. He happily waited for it to be delivered.

Our conversations about music varied. **He** was the guide, **his** were the choices of topics. We talked about different composers, styles of interpretation, music in his childhood, the music of Quebec and many other musical subjects. His life patterns were being changed by the illness and many of his previous activities were now curtailed by increasing weakness. He knew it and tuned into new resources. As a result he lived more fully than any therapist could have hoped.

To date his musical experiences had been of a traditional nature (listening to music, concerts, singing). During a visit, shortly before the piano was to be delivered, I brought up the subject of improvisation, the direct translation of feelings and emotion into sound. At this point our conversation for the first time touched on the seriousness of his illness and the scope of its impact; physical, psychological, social and spiritual. Gérard was a "coper", one of those exceptional persons who, although seriously ill, had learned to appreciate something positive in each day, and used this to accept the sadness, pain and difficulties of other moments. "I haven't spent much time exploring my feelings - I live them," he told me. The thought of expressing them through music so far meant being objective and factual - reproduction of a scene or written notes. "Expression of inner perceptions? - an idea I will have to think about."

By my next visit the piano had arrived. We read through some easy duets in one of his books and he hesitantly joined me in exploring the idea of free improvisation. He participated very reluctantly and I sensed his doubts about such "music" yet didn't comment on it. I was offering him a new resource for expression and renewal that would only prove useful to him if **he** chose to abandon himself to it.

The Christmas Season followed and by the time I returned to visit Gérard, he found it difficult to sit up at the piano. Recorded music filled the gap, and I expanded that experience for him by searching out particular records he did not have in his collection. Recognizing the speed of his increasing weakness I transcribed some records on cassette tapes which could be available on a portable machine at the bedside. Changing records obliged him to get up too frequently.

The advancing illness shifted the focus of my visits. Concerns regarding his will, painful experiences, memories of a previous marriage and the behaviour of his daughter from that marriage dominated his thinking, and he needed to talk about these things. I was a listener he obviously trusted; we had shared the richness, depth and enjoyment of music and now he felt free to share his worries and sorrows, the "inner music" he lived right now.

When he needed admission to the hospital for an abdominal tap and reassessment, I assured the availability of tapes and records in his room, allowing him and his wife to continue living "their world", even though in the hospital.

Gérard died at home. Music remained his comforter and companion to the end, and continues to be the lifeline for Lise, his wife. Without doubt, in this instance, music served as a bridge to the past and the future.

Months later his widow wrote:

> "Music is happiness, in small or large measure, touching suddenly and never failing. And I have come to believe that this is what music meant to him. Music accompanied him to the threshold of death, and he seemed to die peacefully.
>
> "How to find words for music? They are unnecessary - music speaks for itself. In the eight years we lived together music spoke to us of happiness and love; it was a delight we shared, a very special link between us.
>
> "When his illness progressed and we were told that death would probably win over life in the struggle with cancer, music became central. The music therapist brought him an autoharp; an easy, happy instrument which he could play in a comfortable chair or in bed. During the day he learned to accompany Christmas carols which he would sing to our daughter in the evening. When she knew them we would all sing together.

"Gérard wanted to play music, especially the piano, and I remember the Friday night when we managed to get to the store. He told the salesman: 'I'm convalescing and I want to buy a piano. I have plenty of time and want to start playing again.' And so the instrument we had so often talked about arrived at our home. He played as much as he could for about a month. When he couldn't get up to the piano anymore, I started to use it rather clumsily with the help of a teach-it-yourself piano book rather than let him feel the instrument would be abandoned.

"He used to say: 'The great thing with music is that you can enjoy it even when strength fails you.' Now, Bach and Chopin kept him company during all his waking hours in bed. These two composers had a kind of monopoly and I often thought that the sedative power of their music was much stronger than the many pills he had to swallow.

"In December, two months before he died, we managed to go to a harpsichord concert. Out of his bed, into the car, walking from the car to the church, sitting on a hard church bench for a couple of hours - these were great little victories over his disease. The desire to hear just that music had given him renewed energy.

"When he had to be hospitalized, tapes and records, brought by the music therapist, recreated a livable world for him. He refused drugs, using sonatas and symphonies as his sedatives. We would spend an hour or two together, without a word, just holding hands and sharing the music. He was going to die but we were living happiness and peace.

"Back home again, music remained his most faithful support. He, once so talkative, turned into an intense and keen listener. He wanted to keep living as much and well as he could and listening meant living.

"Shortly before his death music gave us the most precious evening of our married life. A musician friend, whom Gérard loved very much but had not seen for over ten years, came to visit. He played for him - songs he liked, melodies that held memories for the two of them, Bach and Chopin, plenty of it. Gérard's face glowed with happiness. Wealth of music, a feast, joy of the world, love, friendship all united in moments when life seemed perfect. Intensity of emotions and invading pain became music, and strange as it seems I don't seem able to think of him without associations to music.

"Two weeks later when he stopped breathing, I spontaneously got up and put on the record of a Beethoven Sonata he had received as a gift the previous week, and this music played until his body was taken from the house. When friends and relatives gathered to remember him and to say goodbye, the music of Susan's flute wove a thread through those moments, a ceremony that couldn't have been different.

"Since then music has helped me to survive. I have started to study the piano seriously, which gives me constant and renewed pleasure. There are no lonely and difficult moments without music as my companion and comforter. Music is also my continued link with him, a link that doesn't hurt but calms moments of intense, almost unbearable pain. The music can't make the pain vanish but it eases it and makes it bearable. Through music I have found the way back to the joy and eagerness for living, which in spite of everything, hadn't quite left me.

"Music never abandons you but you can abandon yourself to it without fear of being destroyed."

Lise Laberge
June, 1982

CASE 2

NOTE AND OBSERVE

- coping mechanisms of the patient, an extension of his normal personality pattern
- some conspiracy of silence in family
- initial goal of music therapy: encourage active/ conscious listening and establish contact
- risk taking by therapist to challenge patient towards continued living
- support through phone contact for wife as patient's condition deteriorates

David, aged 48, married, father of two children, and an accountant was suffering from malignant melanoma. After the initial diagnosis, treatment had given him some months of remission before new symptoms necessitated readmission to the hospital. The PCS home care service began to follow him when he was discharged with the knowledge that further active treatment would not alter the course of the disease.

Work had been David's main interest. With two partners he had set up a consulting firm 2 years prior to diagnosis. Now the illness dramatically curtailed his activity. I was asked to see him to explore the role music might play in helping him to modify his lifestyle and to adjust to the realities of the illness.

On my first visit he was sitting up in bed and seemed very pleased with my presence. On the bedside table lay copies of "An Anatomy of an Illness" (9) and "Getting Well Again" (10). "So you work with music," he greeted me. "Tell me about it," I acknowledged his remark but evaded a lengthy answer by posing a more personal question: "Well, where does music fit into things for you?" This led him to tell me that he enjoyed music at times, but didn't consider himself to be very musical or to have much musical knowledge, "My wife knows much more about music." Listening to a record after coming home from work had helped him to unwind. He didn't seem to have particular preferences, "Nothing too noisy or too heavy ... to tell you the truth I never gave my choices of records much thought."

The conversation turned to his present situation: forced inactivity, uncertainty regarding the future, disappointment, possibly anger. David's facial expression remained unchanged, friendly and smiling, not the slightest trace of emotions that might have matched the issues touched upon. "I'm doing quite well, just have to be a bit patient. No, I'm not disappointed about the relapse. These things can happen." I was aware that the tone of his comments was probably the same he used in a business setting when discussing financial strategies or accounting procedures. Strangely, there seemed to be no difference in his reaction to this conversation around terminal illness.

I related to him ways that music had been helpful to some of the patients with whom I was working, and encouraged David to indulge in more conscious listening with a focus on the nonverbal communication of music. Taking the cue from his choice of books I spoke about the ability of music to reach conscious and unconscious levels of a person and referred to the studies of Helen Bonny and Ruth Savary (11). "I never thought of music in that way, I guess I should try to learn. As you can see, I'm looking into approaches that might help me understand things better."he said pointing at the books on the bedside table. "Where do I start?"

His stereo set was in the living room and he spent most of his time in bed in the bedroom. He had tried to listen to some tapes but wasn't very satisfied with the sound quality of the small portable recorder he used. I happened to have a very small tape recorder and headphones with me. (12) David examined the set and was surprised by the sound quality: "I have seen people jogging with these things on and have seen advertisements about them but I figured they just were another 'gadget'. I think I should buy one! If I have to be in bed I might as well enjoy good sound when listening to music." As his wife wrote a cheque for me to buy such a machine for them, I felt uneasy; would he really use it, and for how long, to justify such an expense? Prolonged illness often stretches family budgets to their limits and this wasn't a small amount to spend. Were any of these questions my business? I had introduced the subject but had no idea he would take it up so readily. I was pleased with his initiative and willingness to explore the idea of becoming an "active" music listener and hoped doors would open to further music therapy developments. Such a sign of initiative was important and especially precious since the future was uncertain. I therefore put aside my uneasiness and focused on the positive aspects of my intervention. Both David and his wife seemed pleased with my visit and ready to accept music as a new dimension in his care.

As I started to leave the house I met David's parents in the living room. They had come across the Pacific when he had been admitted with acute symptoms that seemed lifethreatening at the time. Now the weeks were passing and they wondered if they should stay. They missed their friends, their comfortable habits of daily living. Why had David not written that he was so sick? How could a mole on the leg turn into such a terrible disease? All these concerns spilled out in quiet voices within just a few minutes while David's wife stayed behind in the bedroom. When she joined us in the living room the conversation changed to some casual remarks. They thanked me for coming and invited me to return soon. I left the house pleased with the patient's reactions regarding music therapy, yet very aware of the many unspoken dimensions and issues that would influence future encounters.

Not wanting to let David's enthusiasm for music listening dwindle, I bought the tape recorder the very next day and took it to the house. Things had changed. David had had a restless night, with pain again after some painfree days. Worry was written on the faces of his parents and his wife. The patient looked slightly paler and drawn. Yet, he adamantly denied that this new pain worried him. We unpacked his new "toy", as he called it, and set it up. He seemed pleased, but it was obvious that he was physically uncomfortable and tense. Behind his courteous smiles and comments I sensed an undercurrent of irritability. Given the situation and his unspoken signals I respected his wishes to pretend everything was just fine. I only gently suggested that he might particularly choose some of his quiet music to relax with and left after a short time.

Should I have pursued issues like rhythm and breathing, tension and relaxation, music and supressed feelings, ect? Theoretically, perhaps yes, yet David had clearly given me a message by his behaviour. The message I sensed sounded like: "This is my business. I want (need) to pretend all is well, I appreciate your concern but I want to be left alone right now." I knew if he would let music reach him it would help him more than any therapeutic technique I might offer.

On my next visit I found David sitting in the living room. His mother had coaxed him to get up, which he had only agreed to very reluctantly. She was delighted to see me since she felt slightly guilty for having pushed him into some activity.

He had chosen to sit in a chair right next to the stereo system which led me to invite him to look through his record collection and to give us a "concert". For the next hour we looked through all his records, selected some for taping (one of which, a selection of overtures, we taped right away as we listened to it) and shared many of the memories and anecdotes about trips, friends and happenings connected to some of the music. His wife came back from errands and was obviously happy to see him up and "active". Friends dropped in to visit and joined the "musical tea party". David hadn't been up for such a long period for weeks and visibly enjoyed himself. When he finally got up to go back to bed he was tired but very pleased with the events, as was the rest of the family. I encouraged him to plan a daily taping session in the living room; a goal to work towards, with the additional reward of having his music at the bedside afterwards.

On my next visit, I found David back in bed again. His physical condition didn't seem to have changed yet from his wife's introductory conversation I gathered that he had hardly been out of bed. "I'm comfortable here, I guess I am lazy. I must say I did enjoy the music when you were last here. I got my wife to tape me another cassette." I could appreciate his struggle with increasing weakness, but I also knew that stimulating activity could counteract gradual withdrawal, isolation and immobility. I shared these thoughts with him making sure I did not overlook acknowledging the difficulty of his situation. Having sensed his family's concern regarding his inactivity, and knowing from conversation with his nurse that his physical condition had not changed, I decided to be more direct in my approach: "I appreciate how difficult things are for you, yet I cannot help but feel that what we are really talking about is a matter of choice, to continue living or to wait to die. Neither is easy." There was a tense moment of silence during which I deserately hoped that he had heard my comment as the challenge it was intended to be rather than a reproach. I added: "I feel a bit uneasy saying this for I realize that I can only try to imagine what you must live through." "Don't worry, I really appreciate what you are doing. I wondered myself if I needed to be pushed a bit harder" he answered with a broad smile. Our conversation continued, but I knew that the motivation to participate actively in continued living had to come from within him if it was going to have meaning. I had risked to challenge and now had to wait. If music was going to be a source of pleasure, activity or comfort in that living, **he** had to make that choice.

It now seemed appropriate to suggest ways in which he might use his tapes in bed besides just passive listening. His breathing was very shallow and his body looked tense. We practiced breathing deeply to the rhythm of a quiet piece, and tension/relaxation as well as range of motion exercises to more animated rhythms. When I left, he again expressed appreciation for my having "pushed" him.

A week later it was obvious that David was physically uncomfortable. When I had phoned to announce my visit he had felt a bit better and apparently had surprised everyone by planning to get up once I arrived. An hour later new pain symptoms had dampened his enthusiasm and he was disappointed. He readily accepted the distraction of music from his pain and soon dozed off.

David's condition deteriorated during the following weeks. He had too little energy for visitors and slept for long periods. I left it to his wife to contact me when she felt that my input could be helpful. She called me a few times to keep me up to date on events and seek reassurance that she was doing the right things for her husband. "Maybe you should just come and visit when you can," she said during one call. I heard the unspoken plea, "Please come and share this time with me. I need you as much as David did."

David was admitted to the hospital the day that I planned to visit and died the same evening.

CASE 3

NOTE AND OBSERVE

- home visits may be long, exhausting
- sad, depressed, discouraged patient
- transference of feelings to caregivers
- impact of an unsightly wound
- music therapy may be refused

On the way to join one of the home care nurses at a patient's home, I reviewed the case history of Mrs. Petakis in my mind:

> A 37 year old lady, of Greek origin; cancer of the breast, diagnosed four years ago; left-sided mastectomy at that time; right-sided mastectomy a year ago; reccurances on chest wall despite chemotherapy. Referred to the Palliative Care Service for home care support.
>
> The patient initially had been reticent to accept the nurses' visit but later responded well to the non-threatening support. She stated her main problem was "I think about the disease," and indeed her whole demeanour expressed sadness, depression and lack of motivation. The home care nurse had suggested involving the music therapist and the patient had accepted a visit.

My thoughts continued to wander -- what would I be able to offer? To play for her? To invite her to express through improvisation or to write a song about her preoccupations at this time? What were her physical capabilities now? She had been so hesitant to accept "outsiders". I pulled the car up in front of the house still asking questions yet knowing that I would find answers if I would allow myself to observe and listen without expectations. Kay, the nurse, had arrived a bit earlier, let me in the house and introduced me to Mrs. Petakis who was sitting at the kitchen table. Her mother, puttering near the sink, noded a shy hello. She spoke only Greek.

"You were saying, that you find it harder and harder to relate to the children," said Kay as she picked up the thread of the conversation before my arrival. I sensed how the deep sadness expressed in Mrs. Petakis' face and posture had started to transfer into my feelings. Her voice interrupted my thoughts. "I know they must go on living, I tell them to do so, but when they leave to play hockey or to see friends I just can't help feeling that they have no idea how sick I am. I feel so useless." Her eyes never looked up into ours, her face mirrored hopelessness. Kay, who had met the children, carried on the conversation, gradually drawing me into it. I learned that Mrs. Petakis' twelve year old girl used to take music lessons but lately the patient couldn't tolerate the noise of her practice so the child had stopped lessons. Mrs. Petakis momentarily related that she used to enjoy music, especially Greek dance music, then quickly returned to the burden of her illness, her feelings of uselessness and her aggravation with just about everything. As we sat and talked I wove the idea of music as expression and music for relaxation into the conversation. I picked up on her theme of uselessness, focusing at first on diversion. When I mentioned piano improvisation she smiled for a moment: "Kids play," she said, her voice slightly sarcastic, yet I could tell from her expression that she knew better. "Think of it as diversion, an adventure into the world of imagination and a way to release some of the tension you mentioned earlier," I replied. "I am too sick, too worried, it's no use," she declared. The conversation lingered on, with frequent changes of subject, but the patient agreed to let me come back two days later. We planned to do a collage together.

The nurse still had to change the patient's dressing. Since I was aware of Mrs. Petakis' reluctance to show the oozing lesions on the mastectomy site to the nurse until recently, I offered to wait in the kitchen.

"You can come and help Kay if you wish." To my surprise, Mrs. Petakis invited me. Our sharing in her worries must have given her some support and trust in our motives.

While Kay prepared the materials for compresses and the dressing, I tuned the radio on the night table to some quiet music and showed the patient some tension and relaxation exercises, suggesting that she could use music and relaxation to improve her sleeping patterns. This time there was less resistance on her part. I dared to reflect on the look of disdain that brushed over her face when Kay uncovered the wound saying, "It must be hard to live with this." She nodded holding back tears and then told us how she locked herself in the room, when she changed the dressing so the children wouldn't walk in on her. Once again I was aware of the grief and discouragement the patient felt and how those feelings transfered to Kay and myself. We spoke little yet sensed that Mrs. Petakis was aware of and appreciated our attempt to share her sorrow. She now made more eye contact and smiled once in a while. Her body was less tense. We talked about our plan for music and a collage once more while Kay finished up. The two of us left shortly after, exhausted from the three hour visit, yet optimistic that we had kindled a small flame of new motivation.

Kay phoned the patient the next day to confirm an upcoming appointment at the hospital clinic and during the conversation the patient's husband cancelled my visit for the following day. He stated that his wife had been very upset after our visit and hadn't slept well that night. We wondered what had happened. Was the idea of music too threatening? If so, too threatening for whom - the patient or the husband?

When I related the events to Dr. Boisvert, we planned that he would have a tape recorder and relaxation tapes in the clinic to be "prescribed" for the patient and her husband by the physician.

Mr. and Mrs. Petakis refused the idea of music. They appreciated our support and understood the implications of the therapeutic use of music. But this kind of intervention reminded them how serious the illness was. They used to enjoy dancing but memories were too painful at this time.

CONSIDERATIONS AND OBSERVATIONS ON MUSIC THERAPY IN THE HOME CARE SETTING

To work with a patient in his own environment offers many positive and challenging dimensions. The appearance and "feeling" of an apartment, a room, a house reflects an instant perception of the person's lifestyle, habits and characteristics without much need for questions. A patient's home is a far more intimate setting for music events than the hospital ward with its many noises and interferences. In the security of their familiar surroundings, people usually interact more freely and easily. At the same time, however, individuals have a need to protect and preserve the intimacy of their home, especially in the presence of illness, and can at times be reticent to accept visits from strangers, even health care professionals. We have generally found that nurses rarely encounter such reticence, but they in turn cannot always convince a patient to accept a visit of one of their colleagues from the multidisciplinary team. In each of the preceeding case studies, the music therapist was introduced by the home care nurse on the occasion of the first visit to the patient's house, and this often seems to be the most satisfactory approach. If the patient is known to the music therapist in the hospital, follow-up on home care can continue naturally.

Families usually treat the music therapist as a visitor, extending their usual hospitality. A cup of coffee or tea, a glass of sherry, sampling of some home baked cake or a particular ethnic specialty become vital rituals in the therapeutic relationship. It is often during these moments of informal, comfortable sharing that one comes to understand the family dynamics and concerns, or gains new insights on how to involve the patient in music related activities. The music therapist must learn to feel comfortable on a home visit in which music may have no role to play, where family patterns seem to block suggested activities, or processes begun cannot be continued as planned.

The progression of the illness, the presence of physical symptoms as well as the psychological adjustment of the patient and his family continually fluctuate and demand flexibility in the chosen approaches. In the home setting we need to remind ourselves continually that we are on the patient's very personal territory and realize that our involvement might be perceived as an intrusion. For example; in a hospital setting we possibly wouldn't think twice about rearranging things in a patient's room to maximize a suitable working arrangement for music involvement. But we have to appreciate that moving things in a home might be completely unacceptable to the patient and his family. Such issues are part of family dynamics, which, in the presence of life threatening illness, are often fragile and demand particular respect and sensitivity. Keen awareness, astute observation, patience and tact are particularly essential ingredients in home care work.

FREQUENCY OF VISITS

Each situation dictates a particular pattern of involvement for the palliative care team. The nurse is the pivotal figure in coordinating home care since her visits can be regular and more frequent than those of the music therapist. If a patient isn't feeling well on a particular day he might still want to see the nurse but probably not the music therapist unless a comfortable relationship has already been established and the patient appreciates music interventions as part of the treatment of symptoms. The examples in the preceeding case studies illustrate this issue. The frequency of visits will vary from case to case between a visit per week, to one every two or three weeks. Involvement may be intense for a short time and then be interrupted through the evolution of disease process or other events in the patient's life (eg. hospitalization for palliative treatment, holidays, visitors, etc.)

These realities are at times very taxing on the music therapist who must plan and integrate interventions in already often difficult situations, where continuity is never assured. A consistent focus on small accomplished interventions, and close collaboration with the nurse to keep issues in the total context of each case can help diminish frustrations and feelings of fragmentation.

LENGTH OF VISITS

The average home care visit for the music therapist usually lasts one to two hours. It is rarely possible to arrive at a home and proceed straight to a music therapy activity since the patient or family members often want to talk initially about issues of concern. It is up to the therapist to tune into the situation carefully and set limits should it be that such conversation might be a detour maneuver for avoiding involvement in music.

TYPE OF MUSIC THERAPY ACTIVITY IN HOMECARE

The case studies give some examples of the type of involvement possible. A primary goal will always be to stimulate the patient's initiative and motivation, finding ways in which music will play a role **beyond** the time of the therapist's visit.

To be confined by illness demands modification of lifestyle. A renewed or new interest in music can fill inactive hours. The therapist might suggest:

- community resources, such as libraries (books on music, records, cassettes) local music groups/choirs, concerts (for the still mobile patient)
- cataloguing/taping/reviewing of the patient's music collection (as a legacy for friends or family)
- instrument playing - to pick up where one left off (for someone who used to play) or to begin from scratch on an instrument that won't demand years of learning (if that is something the person used to wish for)
- exploration in guided imagery
- drawing, painting or creating collages stimulated by music
- free improvisation or expression of feelings, emotions and concerns
- song or poetry writing

The patient's physical status at the time of involvement will determine possible activities. On the other hand, his/her emotional and psychological adjustment to a lifethreatening illness as well as the pre-existing attitudes towards creative involvement and expression will greatly influence readiness and openness towards music therapy.

In the case of Gerard, he had consciously "lived" music before he was ill. He adapted his lifestyle and continually tried to find new meaning in the difficult adjustments forced on him by progressing disease. When the time was right he felt comfortable sharing his deeper thoughts and painful feelings. For the music therapist, as well as the nurse, he was an unusual patient to work with, stimulating our search for personal growth and facilitating our interventions. Patients with advanced malignant disease who retain attitudes and openness as illustrated by Gerard are the exceptions.

David remained reserved, business-like, "locked-in", except for the occasional moment, not only towards us but also towards his friends and family. When the therapist risked challenging him into continued living, it was evident that he tried to cope with the reality of an adjusted lifestyle intellectually, yet remained restricted by preoccupations with symptoms, unexpressed thoughts, feelings and daily routines. This was **his** way of dealing with his illness, which needed to be respected. Those around him found it difficult to share. It was important that the therapist continue supportive contact by phone with the wife when David became too withdrawn and ill to want to be involved in music, and not abandon her at her most difficult time.

INVOLVEMENT IN THE FACE OF PROGRESSING DISEASE

In the work with the terminally ill, the continued involvement of the music therapist, once the patient's condition has deteriorated beyond the ability to actively participate, is particular to this setting and often essential. As weakness increases and verbal communication diminishes or ceases, the non-verbal communication of music can take on precious dimensions. For example; the mother of a young brain tumor patient who had not verbally responded for weeks took great comfort in observing her son's facial expression light up when music was played for him. The music therapist's role, once having introduced the idea of using music at certain times during each day, was to nurture the mother's involvement in this "new kind of care," to help her select appropriate music and to guide her in using music for her own comfort and renewal as well. When the therapist visited, most of the time was spent with the mother who needed to share her feelings of pain, sadness and grief regarding the impending loss of her son. Although she felt that her physical care could not reach him anymore she now was certain that the music was reaching to his "inner being" and soul, giving her a renewed sense of closeness to him.

Another patient who had enjoyed singing and playing the piano with the therapist until breathing difficulties and generalized weakness curtailed this activity, continued to live her music through the therapist's playing of previously shared melodies. She was able to compensate for her loss by taking pleasure in the music, even though she could no longer be the active musician.

Many patients, however, find music intolerable as they see themselves weaken and death approaches. They will need the assurance that the therapist understands and respects their feelings, and continues to care, regardless. On some occasions families will ask for music to be played again during the last few hours of the person's life. These are precious moments where music transcends emotional, physical and spiritual barriers.

To work with a patient in the intimacy of his/her home is a privilege which allows the therapist to witness and share the difficulties, joys, tensions, worries, defeats and triumphs of the struggle with terminal illness more closely than in the hospital setting. Here, the patient and the family are in charge and make decisions that demand respect and tolerance. They take the risk of exposing their vulnerability and their idiosyncracies at a very trying time in their life. This in turn places a serious responsibility on the shoulders of the therapist, who in this setting often has to face personal vulnerability, fears and professional challenges without the support of other health care team members. There is no place to "slip into a role" or to perform learned patterns in the setting of a home. The challenge of each home care case pushes the therapist towards a search for new dimensions of music therapy and brings confrontation with feelings of frustration, helplessness and inadequacy. Each case does offer the richness of intimate sharing in the very essence of human interaction brought into focus by impending death.

CONSULTATION

CASE 1

NOTE AND OBSERVE

- patient's denial despite full insight
- verbal/non-verbal communication
- therapist's feelings of uncertainty with risks, limits, approaches
- music counteracts insomnia, later becomes medium for relaxation
- collage technique helps to get in touch with past unresolved grief

Dr. Boisvert met me in the hall as he returned to the office from a consultation visit to a patient in one of the hospital pavilions, "I would like you to see this patient," he said and gave me a short case history:

> 51 year old lady with rapidly progressive lung cancer. Had pneumonectomy 6 months ago followed by radiotherapy which "washed her out." Lost 25 lbs., recovered and felt well until two months ago, when she developed hip pain. Now admitted for hip pinning. Extremely anxious and tense.
>
> Patient has full knowledge of illness. Angry at God and bargaining for more time to raise her twelve year old daughter. Husband and one son (age 28) very supportive.
>
> Patient lost both parents when she was about 10, all brothers dead, four sisters living, who are supportive as well.

A couple of hours later I went to see Mrs. Kunz. "Hello Mrs. Kunz, I'm Susan Munro, the music therapist from the Palliative Care Service. Dr. Boisvert sent me to see you." The patient slowly and uneasily shifted position, obviously very uncomfortable and restless. "Hello! Yes, Dr. Boisvert was here a while ago. I don't know what's the matter with me. I'm so uncomfortable." Her eyes filled with tears, which she tried to suppress and wipe away hastily, "I can't sleep, and I'm in so much pain."

"Let the tears run, it is all right to cry. It must be tough to be sick like this." Silence! The tears rolled quickly down the patient's face. I gently put my hand on her arm for a few moments and the quiet tears turned into uncontrolled sobs. The minutes passed, the sobs subsided and looking at me with a faint smile Mrs. Kunz broke the silence, "I'm sorry I'm such a crybaby. I've always cried easily but now ... I just can't believe what's happening. I thought I was all right again. Last summer I had an operation on my lungs. It was terrible. I was so sick. They gave me radiotherapy, and I vomited all the time. I didn't want to eat anymore and I lost 30 pounds. I never thought one could feel this low! Well, eventually things picked up and by November I started to feel really well again until this pain in my hip appeared. I tried to ignore it, thinking it might be arthritis, but it got worse. On New Year's Eve I saw my doctor because I couldn't stand the pain anymore and here I am. They tell me I have a hole in my bone, and they will have to put a pin in to stengthen it. I'm so nervous I can't relax!" Tears welled up again.

All these remarks came out as broken statements, abrupt outbursts with intermissions of silence. I didn't interrupt but listened and observed, my posture and facial expression communicating full attention and understanding sympathy.

I observed that Mrs. Kunz kept shifting restlessly in bed. I noticed the tension in her body and face, the fleeting eye contact and the changing facial expression. I heard the intensity of her voice changing with the flow of her feelings as she related events and I realized that the word "cancer" was carefully avoided. Yet it hung heavily in the air, fanning the patient's anxiety.

"You have been through a lot, no wonder you're so upset" and changing my voice to a rather matter of fact nonchalant tone I went on: "Tell me, do you like music?" Instantly she looked straight at me with a puzzled look (I could almost read the unspoken "you must be crazy" in her eyes). The restless fidgeting stopped for just a moment and a mischievious smile spread across her face: "How did you know?" I answered, "Well, music has a place in most people's lives; for some a big place, for others just a small corner." The atmosphere in the room had changed. For the first time in over 30 minutes her focus shifted away from symptoms and illness. "At home I always had the radio on, especially before I was sick." "Any favourites?" "Humperdinck and Tom Jones" came a direct, firmly spoken answer without hesitation.

"I noticed your bewildered look when I mentioned music a couple of minutes ago. I guess you thought this to be rather inappropriate when you were feeling so badly, which is understandable. But look, you've just been able to forget your worries for a minute. Music has a way of carrying off our minds. I'd like to bring you a tape recorder and some of your favourites on tapes if you let me. They might take your mind off your worries and help you think of other things!"

"I really haven't felt like music for awhile now!"

"I'm not surprised. Still, I'd like to bring you the equipment and then you have it on hand of you feel like it. Remember the saying 'L'appetit vient en mangeant!' The tape recorder won't mind if you turn it off!"

"If you think so."

"Thank you, I'll go and get the things right now."

On my return, some 15 minutes later, I was greeted with a smile. I set up the machine within easy reach of the patient and showed her how to manipulate it, puffed up her pillows and helped her settle comfortably in bed. I could feel her body rigid with anxiety as I did so, but realized that she was still too tense to hear suggestions of relaxation techniques. "Would you like me to leave the music on now?" I asked casually, leaving the decision to the patient. "Well, I guess so," she answered tentatively. I selected the Humperdinck tape which she quickly recognized, adjusted the volume to an unintrusive level, said goodbye and left.

One day later: As I entered Mrs. Kunz's room she immediately turned off the television and greeted me with a big smile. "I feel so much better, I fell asleep when you left yesterday and I had such a good night's sleep, the first in a long time. Dr. Boisvert had said he was going to change my medication. That is what must have made the difference! (wouldn't it be nice to have had a way of measuring the music's contrubution in this matter, mused my music therapist's mind). Mind you, I still feel very tense. They are going to pin my hip tomorrow. I just can't believe it! I don't want to suffer again like I did last summer. I want to go away,

I need a break. I have had enough!'' As she spoke, her voice had quickly changed to an anxiety pitch once more and she began shifting uneasily in the bed again. ''Things might not be as bad this time. Tell me, do you have records at home? I have no Tom Jones in my tapes here and you mentioned him as your other favourite singer.''

''Yes, we do have some records.''

''If someone in your family could bring them in, I can tape them for you. Being in the hospital might then be a bit more like home! Is your family able to visit often?''

''My husband comes every day after work. My son is away for the moment, and I don't want my daughter to come during the week when she has school and lots of homework.'' Her voice quivered and she turned away, shifting position in bed.

''Do you think your husband would bring the records in? With the operation tomorrow it will be important to keep you in music so you can sleep!!! I also would like to bring you some special tapes I have prepared for relaxation.'' (13)

''No, no I don't think I'll feel like music. Anyway, I'm scared and worried!''

She began to cry. I put my hand gently on her arm, remaining silent for awhile, then said quietly, ''It's really hard isn't it!'' She nodded and dried her face. ''Look, yesterday you fell asleep when you least expected it and you felt better this morning. That might not seem like much but it is at least something positive to hang onto right now that everything seems so gloomy.''

My remark hung in the air, I sensed that the patient weighed this thought with little conviction. I felt the weight of her sadness, grief and tears. We exchanged a few more words and I left, keenly aware of a sense of failure. Should I have pushed the issue of relaxation music? Should I have just come with my flute and ''spoken'' with music rather than words? I remembered her look of incredibility when I even mentioned music. Could classical music give her comfort? My thoughts raced on. I realized how the reality of cancer, its symptoms, its uncertainties, and unpredictabilities invade not only the patient's body but also the mind and the minds of those in contact with the patient as well.

When I later met one of the consulting nurses on our team, I mentioned that Mrs. Kunz had slept better. I remarked to my colleague ''Of course, she attributes it to Dr. Boisvert changing of medications! I want to believe it was the music that broke the vicious circle of preoccupation with her symptoms!'' Together we went and checked the drug records of the previous evening. The physician's orders had not been carried out! She had received the same medications as on previous nights!

The next few days the patient's focus was on post-operative treatment. I made a couple of short visits to bring her the records her husband had lent me and the tapes. I sensed that we were starting to settle into a relationship of trust and now dared to bring the relaxation tapes along, introducing her to these at the end of one of my short visits.

Mrs. Kunz's pinned hip was healing well but she felt a new pain in the upper abdomen. Her anxiety reached new peaks. She could focus only on this new pain but had started to use the relaxation tapes on her own and found them helpful.

By now I could talk more freely with her for the music created a kind of a bond between us. Her conversations were full of unspoken fears, but the word ''cancer'' was still avoided. I started using it gently and periodically. I introduced the idea of painting/drawing to music to the patient, who, when left with cassettes, paper and pastels, ventured into this activity. Shyly she showed me some of her drawings -- trees, flowers, clouds and an airplane. "I want to go away. If I only could go to the sun, to a beach, to Florida then I would be all right again. It is crazy! I am so afraid of planes, but right now I would get on one without thinking." Her eyes filled with tears again and she looked away. "I would be all right again".

I repeated reflectively, "I think I hear you saying that what's happening to you is like a nightmare; you hope you will wake up and find it isn't true -- yet you know that all of this is really happening to you, don't you."

She slowly nodded her head, crying. "I can imagine that you are confronted by so many conflicting feelings that it must be very difficult to try to sort them out right now." Again she nodded. "I would like you to do a collage to music with me. We will leaf through magazines while we listen to some music and will cut out any pictures that strike us as matching the music. Then we will arrange these on a large piece of paper. This can be a way to project issues which preoccupy us into a picture. We can then look at this picture with a new objectivity and possibly gain fresh understanding. Shall we do this tomorrow?"

"If you think so," she answered doubtfully.

"I'll be here around eleven then. Think of it as an adventure and you needn't worry all night!"

The next day I found the patient up in a chair waiting for me. I spread out magazines, scissors and glue, prepared the tape recorder and started the music. (14) I sat on the empty bed and began working on a collage of my own, observing Mrs. Kunz out of the corner of my eye.

She began to tear and cut out pictures very quickly, without hesitation, seeming very absorbed. She arranged and glued them on the paper and finished minutes after the music stopped. As I turned to look at her collage, she smiled, held it slightly away from her and started pointing at the pictures: "I like pretty things; like this table, good food, good company, being happy." Then her voice changed and the words spilled out quickly and full of tension. "I want to go away on a trip, to the country, to a beach ... I have gone through so much ... I can't go on ... I need some rest," she said as she turned the picture over and pointed to the sofa picture. "I want to take the plane!" These last words came with a sudden chuckle, as she seemed to remember our conversation of the previous day. "Escape?" I reflected. Slowly she turned the paper back to the front glancing over the pictures once more. We both knew she had not mentioned the two very small pictures yet. "That's illness," she added after a moment's silence, her voice full of disdain, "Well , at least I haven't lost my hair yet." In the silence of the next moment I pointed my finger without saying anything to the small circle showing the face of a crying child. "A child crying for help," she said with a shakey voice.

"Your child?"

She began to sob bitterly. I got up and stood beside her putting my arm around her shoulders. "That is one of your biggest worries, isn't it? Do you want to talk about it?"

Over the next twenty minutes words poured out. Her father died in an accident when she was ten and her mother died suddenly when she was twelve. She missed her parents bitterly but she was never encouraged to talk about it. When her daughter was born sixteen years after her son, she worried during the delivery that her girl might have to face the same fate, a premonition that now seemed to come true.

I listened for a long time. Later, we were able to look at the reality of her situation, focus on the importance of being honest about feelings, reflect on including the family in her grief and her illness rather than pretending and hiding behind silence. Even if she should die, her daughter need not go through the same trauma.

The words cancer and death gradually became a natural part of her conversation without the previous signs of agitation.

For another two weeks I visited the patient three times a week. The music was less important now, as she listened to it for pleasure and diversion. I included classical tapes in the selection since she enjoyed the Mozart piece on the relaxation tape. She was knitting a vest for her daughter, hoping to finish it before she could go home.

Our visits were "talking visits" now. The moment I entered the room, the television or radio went off, and the patient seemed to be waiting to share the insights she was slowly gaining. There was still anxiety, but she recognized it and tried to face it instead of putting it out of her mind. Tears were less frequent by this time and I was aware of her more positive outlook. Side effects from the radiotherapy were minimal.

As her discharge from the hospital approached she made plans about coping at home. She sent her son to buy the "relaxation record" (13) as she called it and thought about talking openly with her family. A couple of days before the discharge, her son contacted the consultation nurse to inquire if his mother was receiving anti-depressant drugs since he had never before known her in so positive an attitude. The nurse replied that such drugs had not been necessary!

CASE 2

NOTE AND OBSERVE

- recent diagnosis
- withdrawal, hostility, anger
- importance of patience, waiting
- patient/therapist bond established through sharing of music

A fever, night sweats and some chest pains over a period of three weeks led Mr. Sanchez' family physician to ask for a hospital admission to investigate these persisting symptoms.

Only one month before this admission to the hospital the patient had returned from a three week holiday in his native Spain, tanned, happy and in apparent good physical health.

Extensive tests were carried out, interrupted by hospital holidays, before the diagnosis was finally confirmed. During this time the patient felt vulnerable and neglected.

When he was told of the seriousness of his condition -- poorly differentiated adenocarcinoma, probably of the lung -- the patient refused to believe the diagnosis, becoming very hostile and withdrawn. He blamed the hospital for not finding the cause of what he suspected to be an infection. He stated angrily "All they looked for was cancer." His pain was difficult to control and he scarcely ate. The Palliative Care Consultation team was asked to visit him to help with symptom control. Subsequently the team's physician requested the involvement of the music therapist.

When I entered his private room, Mr. Sanchez had his back to the door. He was a tall man, taking up the full length of the bed, and had pulled the covers as high as he could to hide most of his head. He didn't bother changing positions as I went to the bedside. When I pulled up a chair to sit near him I was very uncomfortably aware that he considered me an intruder. His partially covered face spelled hostility.

"You're having a rough time," I said reflectively into the silence, and as I looked at his now pale face it was difficult to imagine that he had, until just recently, been a picture of health. Still not changing position he nodded slightly "You must be very upset and frustrated".... Silence.

After a few moments he slowly turned and faced me and without much change of expression haltingly talked about the incidents of the last few weeks, alluding to the possibility of his being this sick because of neglect. I listened, making sure to give him full attention, knowing that there was little I could say at this time that might comfort him. Everything was still too new, too overwhelming.

"I wonder if you like music? This might be a strange question for you at this moment, but at times when we feel sad and upset music can speak and comfort where words cannot. I notice you come from Spain and know that music plays an important part in your culture.

"That's true, but now I'm sick and you probably don't have the music I like anyway!"

"I tell you what, I'll bring you a tape recorder and some cassettes for the time being, and then if you feel like using the equipment it's here. I'll understand if you don't feel like listening to music, but the days here must be long when you're waiting for further news on treatments and tests, you may want to ask your wife to bring in some of your own music for you to have at hand. **You** choose when you feel like listening."

I still felt very unwelcome, Mr. Sanchez shivered slightly so I found him an extra blanket and helped him to reposition himself better in the bed. I made sure things on his bedside table were accessable to him and refilled the glass with fresh water. I wanted him to sense that I cared, regardless of his behavior.

A while later I brought him the promised equipment and set it up. He watched me without saying a word, his face stony and full of contempt, his countenance seeming to say "Music!? I am so sick I need a doctor who can get me better and out of here!" I left the room feeling wretched and wondering if I had aggravated him even more. In view of his recent diagnosis, the sudden onset of illness and his background he might have perceived my intervention as insult added to injury.

The following day he was even less communicative. He kept his sheets drawn well over his ears, his eyes turned to the wall. Occasionally he glanced at me as I sat with him for a while. I didn't mention the music or ask questions. He knew who I was and would give the signals if he wanted to pursue the issue of music. He mentioned that things around him were again just as inaccessable as the day before, and rearranging his bedside environment to his liking made me feel just a bit less helpless and inadequate.

A couple of days later he told me he didn't like the music I had brought him since it wasn't what he listened to at home (I had given him five cassettes: Spanish music and a selection of well-liked classics and popular music). I realized quickly that despite his stated dislike he had listened to all five cassettes from beginning to end! He now talked about the music he liked and agreed to let me call his wife to bring in some of his own cassettes. In the meantime he didn't want anything to do with music! His abruptness still made me feel uneasy, and I needed to remind myself that it was **his initiative** that counted in this situation.

He remained hostile towards everyone who came in contact with him. Symptom control was still inadequate and he simply told the Palliative Care Service physician he did not want to see him.

I kept visiting him regularly, respecting his wish not to pursue music issues. I observed that his wife had brought tapes, but since he didn't mention anything I made no comment. We often sat in silence. All I seemed to be able to do for him was to help him reposition comfortably and to arrange the bedside table to his liking.

One day, about two weeks after our last music conversation he broke the silence during my visit. The edge of hostility was gone from his voice as he said: "Would you like to hear **my** music?" He turned and pushed the button of the tape recorder which he had prepared before I arrived. For the next half hour we shared a journey of transformation, beauty, images and feelings. We traveled together with the melodies, sounds, tensions and resolutions and in his music he let me see and feel with him his vulnerability, gentleness, suffering and despair. Through music we moved from being strangers to friends.

When the tape ended he began to talk about his home town: Aranjuez, ("his" music was the Concerto De Aranjuez by Rodrigo), his family, his mother, his illness, his shattered dreams, his frustrations, his fears. I mostly listened; there were few or no answers to many of his questions, and we both knew it. Nevertheless, just to raise the questions seemed to ease his anxiety. I asked his permission to share parts of our conversation with my colleagues on the palliative care team and to involve them more closely in his care, to which he agreed.

With the efforts of the whole team and the treating physicians his symptoms could be controlled enough to allow him to be discharged six weeks later. Over the next nine months he was admitted to the hospital for three more short periods of about two weeks each.

During those admissions he tended to remain distant and withdrawn. His family as well as the staff found it extremely difficult to reach him and to communicate with him. Music only occasionally had any significance for him during these months. The bond between us, however, created in the initial sharing of his music, helped him allow me to keep opening doors when he tried to shut everyone out. Still, he never did accept his illness, and as he saw himself deteriorate, he withdrew further and further into himself.

CASE 3

NOTE AND OBSERVE

- an exceptional patient, open to music therapy and creative adventures
- role of music beyond hospitalization period
- nurturing of healing forces through creative endeavor

When Gabrielle realized she had become jaundiced she gave up her apartment, sold her furniture and car, made arrangements to have her two girls placed in foster homes and admitted herself to the hospital to die. She had seen her mother become jaundiced of cancer and die.

Her physician suggested one more attempt at chemotherapy and the palliative care physician, consulted for pain and symptom control, suggested music therapy among other things to help her cope with the magnitude of emotional and physical dimensions of her illness. She had always liked music and welcomed me warmly when I came to see her. Her bed was in a four-bed room, and she found it extremely difficult to watch her fellow-patients struggle with pain and restlessness. Gabrielle was weak and very ill, able neither to eat nor sleep. Events of the past few weeks had left her quite vulnerable, tense and full of fear. She readily accepted the idea of using headphones to abandon herself to music in the hope of finding comfort.

She later said: "I started listening to music day and night, Bach, Beethoven, Chopin. In the evening and later it was always Chopin (a tape of all of his Etudes). When listening to his music I felt the same emotions I remembered from childhood, when someone held and rocked me. I think that if one is very ill one wishes to be a child again, to be taken care of. Maybe I identified with the emotions the composer tried to express in his music. I dared to let go, I cried a lot and felt better for it, and soon I started to relax and allow myself to sleep."

When I visited her she welcomed the opportunity to talk, for the music had helped her to identify the struggles and conflicts. One of the recurring themes was fear — fear of the unknown, fear of pain. I brought art materials and encouraged her to draw fear. Again she was able to abandon herself to this new activity even though she had never drawn or painted before.

"Look at my fear. It's like a twisted monster!" she said as she showed me her drawing of twisted spider-like blue and black lines. "This is how it should be," she commented as she produced a second, now sun-like picture. Daily she continued to talk, listen to music and draw, gaining more insight into her feelings and reactions. With increased relaxation and sleep she began to eat again. A month and a half after her final admission she was discharged into a convalescent home. I suggested she should take the tape recorder and tapes with her.

"That suggestion was such a relief. I knew I would need it to keep my soul, spirit and mind occupied. I had always worked, and to see myself inactive made me feel useless. Yet, with the music I knew that there were still things I could do while being very sick," she recorded on a tape prepared recounting her illness.

"Fear"

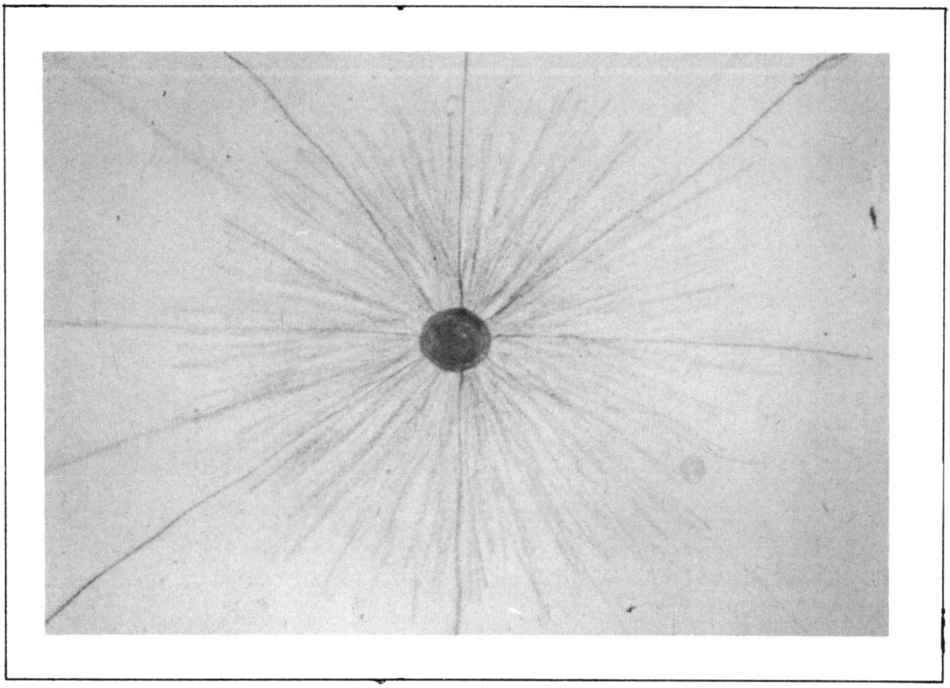

"It Should Be Like This"

"Gabrielle's Life Circle"

In the following months she came to see me each time she was in the hospital for chemotherapy or check-ups. She would exchange the tapes and share her experiences. We enlarged a very beautiful drawing she had made of a "life circle" which she worked into a mural of sculptured wool during the unsuing weeks. When she felt better the music became less important to her. She developed new painting and collage techniques, continuing to surprise herself, her children, friends and the palliative care team with her talents.

From the convalescent home she moved back to a furnished apartment and four months later began part-time work again. When she had pain or symptom problems she would contact us for advise and adjustments in medication and each time music moved into focus again.

The course of her illness defied all medical predictions. She used each day to search for new meaning and goals. When things were difficult she found new strengths in music "I let Chopin rock me - I seemed to hear his music say - let go, feel what you feel, you will be better for it afterwards! I think that without the music and all it has meant to me the chemotherapy wouldn't have had the same effect!"

Gabrielle died two years after her final admission. Three months prior to her death she had enrolled in art classes! Creative experience through music and art had helped her renew her life forces, find new perspectives and grow to new heights.

CASE 4

NOTE AND OBSERVE
- isolation of patient due to disfigurement
- non-verbal communication
- spiritual dimensions of music

Mrs. Moore's face and head, except part of a cheek and her mouth, was covered by a large bandage hiding an ugly tumor which had invaded her eyes and part of her nose. She was half-sitting in her bed, whimpering when I came into her room. I went to her bedside, took her hand, and introduced myself as the music therapist. She didn't respond ... just continued to whimper.

In her chart I had noted that she loved music and used to sing in a church choir. I quietly began to sing a well-known hymn. The moment I began singing her whimpering stopped, her hand searched across the sheets for mine, and she hung on to it tightly while her lips mouthed some of the words. I kept on singing, and she acknowledged each new hymn tune with a squeeze of my hand, her lips moving occasionally to the words. Gradually, as she settled more comfortably into her pillow, her covered face seemed to find composure and peace. The hymns had transformed the hospital room into a sacred place filled suddenly with an inexplainable divine presence. A nurse opened the door, came in, stopped and observed for a moment, then quietly turned and closed the door.

Some moments later I stopped singing and we sat in silence. When I got up to leave she squeezed my hand once more and quietly said "Thank you." She died the next day.

CASE 5

NOTE AND OBSERVE

- crisis intervention
- importance of therapist's familiarity with nursing skills
- lack of background information is handicap
- nurse's retreat to "learned behavior" in death situation
- death event
- staff support

I was about to leave one of the hospital wards when a nurse, who had observed me working with a patient some weeks before, stopped me, asking that I see Mr. Gardener. Her plea sounded urgent so I went to the room without reviewing the chart.

The man was sitting on the side of the bed, his mucus-stained hospital shirt askew and an oxygen mask hanging around his neck. His breathing was very laboured, and he restlessly shifted position trying to get comfortable, almost sliding off the bed with each movement. He simply stared at me with big frightened eyes as I approached. How to think of music at that moment! I wheeled the bedside table in front of him, put a pillow on top and helped him rest his arms on it to keep from sliding off the bed. I placed his feet on a footstool for support before wiping some of the mucus from his face and readjusting his oxygen mask. He pointed at my watch and then mimicked an injection.

The nurse in charge of medications told me that the last injection was given just fifteen minutes ago and they were trying to get in touch with the palliative care physician to question drug dosage. Her comments alluded to differences of opinion between physicians. Increased dosage might mean depression of the patient's already limited respiratory functions. She sounded frustrated, tense and was obviously very concerned about the rapidly deteriorating condition of Mr. Gardener.

I returned to the bedside and reassured the patient that efforts were under way to supplement medication to ease his discomfort. Again he just stared at me very frightened and gasping for air, his body tense and restless. This wasn't a time for conversation and, given the respiratory difficulty, it was difficult to assess how aware his mind was at this stage. I decided to risk bringing relaxation tapes and headphones without his consent in the hope that the soothing rhythm of music might transmit some calm and comfort to him.

Twenty minutes later the scene was still the same, the man's color a bit poorer, the oxygen mask once again covered with bloodstained mucus, his legs extremely edemetous with very taught skin. Across the room a patient had turned up the volume of his radio, obviously trying to drown out the labored breathing of his roommate.

I installed the tape recorder, checked the volume of the relaxation tape (13) through the headphone and gently placed them on his head. I audibly inhaled and exhaled following the rhythm of the music, stood quietly beside Mr. Gardener with my hand on his arm. Two or three minutes later I sensed a change, a slight easing of tension in his body, a bit less fear in his eyes.

"I would like to reposition you so that your legs can rest better. I will keep the head of the bed up to make breathing easier." When I had made the same suggestion on my first visit, he had adamantly refused to move. Now there was a slight nod. I started to prepare the cushions, wondering how best to reposition this heavily set man. At that moment one of the consultation nurses from the Palliative Care Service walked in. She assessed the situation immediately and without talking we proceeded to shift his body into a half-sitting position in the bed. By now his body felt limp and heavy. On observing the patient we both also became aware that he would not live much longer. While we were repositioning him, a woman had walked into the room and now stood some six feet from the bed watching us with a questioning and frightened look. Who was she? His wife, or a relative, or a friend who had come for a visit? What went through her mind as she saw us settling this patient wearing headphones comfortably into the pillows? Neither my colleague nor I knew the patient or his case well, since we had been called only hours before to intervene in this crisis. We were painfully aware of the lack of information in this delicate situation. The patient's breathing had by now slowed to near normal and his eyes were closed.

The nurse went over to the visitor, introduced the two of us and, realizing this was the patient's wife, quickly brought her up to date on the happenings of the last few hours. "I think he is dying now," she said quietly as she ushered Mrs. Gardener to the bedside. A nurse from the floor came in. She took one look at the patient, rushed to the bedside, motioned me impatiently out of the way, clumsily took the man's bloodpressure, turned, and rushed out without saying a word. We never saw her again!

During the next few minutes we stood in silence. Janet, my colleague, had put her arm around Mrs. Gardener's shoulder and gently encouraged her to take her husband's hand in hers. She looked stunned and frightened. The silences between the patient's breaths grew longer, and a little later he quietly stopped breathing. His face was peaceful. After some moments, I removed the headphones and the oxygen mask, rolled down the head of the bed and went over to Mrs. Gardener, suddenly feeling very uneasy. The music had brought calm, but had it precipitated things? Dying with music might seem "good dying" in **my** perception, but what was the the significance for this woman who just lost her husband? This unfortunately, wasn't the time to talk or ask many questions.

The floor staff, who obviously knew Mrs. Gardener, had by now come in and were taking over. Someone ushered her to a telephone booth. A physician drew the curtain around the patient's bed to examine the body. Janet and I walked off the floor back to our office. As suddenly as we had been plunged into the middle of this intense experience we were now totally removed.

We sat and reviewed the events of the last couple of hours, both very grateful for the other's support. We were glad Mr. Gardener hadn't died gasping for air in the presence of his wife. The few quiet moments at the bedside in the midst of the hustle of an active medical ward had seemed very precious, and we both felt privileged to have been there.

In the ensuing weeks, I often thought about this case, wondering exactly what role music had played in the final minutes of Mr. Gardener's life and what his wife's reaction had been. Four months later I received a card from her which answered some of my questions. It read:

> "The help you gave meant such a lot, and, hopefully, you'll know this comes with lots more gratitude than words could ever show.
>
> I enclose a cheque for the use of music therapy in memory of my husband whom you visited in his greatest need at the time of death and you were also of tremendous help to me."

Sincerely,

Emily Gardener

CASE 6

NOTE AND OBSERVE

- long pain history before diagnosis
- Palliative Care Service involvement initially strictly for medical pain control, which eventually left very short time span for palliative care (5 days)
- quality of life = have sister present and piano in room

For a year and a half Mr. Belanger, a widower aged 49, had been plagued by epigastric pain. Because various investigations for a suspected ulcer or other possible diagnoses had all proven negative, his pain was thought to be of psychosomatic origin. He was referred to psychiatry. The psychiatrist, however, concluded that the pain had to be of physical origin and the symptoms of depression and sadness which the patient by now exhibited were appropriate in the face of his long pain history.

Finally, further extensive investigations located an adenocarcenoma of the head of the pancreas and a gastroenterostomy was performed, followed by radiotherapy. The post-operative period was marked by repeated hematemesis and chronic, quite sever pain. The palliative care physician was consulted, but initially **strictly** for medical pain control. Only when it became obvious that any further gastrointestinal bleeding might cause Mr. Belanger's death, and the patient had been informed of this fact, was it possible to involve the extended consultation team.

The patient was very distraught and reflected with bitterness on the physical and mental anguish of his pain history, which now suddenly had brought him to the threshold of death. His biggest wish was to be pain-free. Concerted efforts on the part of the medical team helped to improve pain control to some extent and a family conference initiated by the consultation nurse helped to ease his tension and despair. The conference also revealed his love of music. His sister used to play the piano in their family home.

I offered to move the piano into his private room and fortunately the ward staff made no objections. When he asked me to play for him, I reflected his journey through pain and suffering to him in an improvisation. This communication deeply moved him and allowed him to verbalize still more of his inner anguish.

The piano stayed in the room. I left tapes and a tape recorder as well. The entry in his chart for the following day, December 10, read: "...patient appears in pleasant mood. Sister with him all day playing piano, listening to music. Quite talkative, no mention of illness."

The next day he was also particularly touched when one of the physicians sat down and played especially for him. He died December 13th.

CONSULTATION SERVICE: CONSIDERATIONS FOR THE MUSIC THERAPIST

As it was stated in the overview of the Palliative Care Service, the consultation team plays a central role in the coordination of the complex services of the hospital at large, the PCS' Homecare Service and the Palliative Care Inpatient Unit.

The transition from active anti-cancer treatment to palliative care is often unclear, quite difficult and demands constant review of therapeutic goals and adaptation to each patient's needs and reactions. Health care teams throughout the hospital are trained to focus on investigation, diagnosis, prolongation of life and cure. They often find it difficult or impossible to shift this focus in the face of progressive malignant disease and its impact on everyone involved. It is therefore not unusual to encounter some hostility from some members of certain ward teams when the PCS consultation team is involved with one of **their** patients. These individuals may consider the palliative care philosophy as **giving up** . Perhaps they feel threatened by their own impotence in conquering the disease. The music therapist needs to be aware of these difficulties and potential reactions since on occasion he/she can easily be the target of such hostility. The presence of music or even a music therapist on an active treatment floor is, after all, very unusual, especially in a teaching hospital.

The Palliative Care Consultation team often becomes initially involved at a crisis point in the evolution of the patient's disease; i.e. when surgery reveals advanced inoperable tumour, when symptoms are difficult to control, when traditional therapies fail, when patients withdraw, when families don't seem to be able to cope with the impending death of a loved one. To join with other teams in the care of the patient at such times demands particular sensitivity, tact and diplomacy. It is therefore essential that the music therapist be an integral member of the palliative care team and be kept well-informed of the frequently changing total case picture.

Involvement with these patients comes at various stages of illness: at the time of diagnosis or relapse, at the occurence of new symptoms, at the pre-terminal stage. Each individual cancer history, each different tumor site, the variation in symptom patterns, the age, personality and background of each patient, each family constellation and the perception and attitudes of each treatment team play a part in the complex mesh of circumstances that face the palliative care team. No two cases are ever alike, even though two patients might have the same diagnosis, similar ages and backgrounds. While this may also be true for other pathologies, it is particularly significant in the case of advanced malignant disease. The challenge of meeting the multi-faceted needs of a patient who faces impending death can only be met with a focus on and respect for the uniqueness of each individual.

The medical team usually has detailed information of all pathological and medical data and varying knowledge of the individual's social background and personal life history. Yet in terminal care, the dimensions of innermost feelings, unique perceptions and total personhood may totally alter the symptom picture. Music can be a master key for tuning into this individual uniqueness, because each person's preferred music reflects dimensions of the individual's inner being, feelings, perceptions and lifestyle.

In some instances the only contribution the music therapist can make to the care of a patient is to reveal the "Music person" — defined in a conversation about music or in the sharing of a musical memory or fragments of a tune or words to a song — to the rest of the team. While music might never play a further part in the case, heightened awareness of the patient's framework of thought, emotions and reactions can provide a crucial piece in the puzzle of symptom control to physicians and nurses. If a patient accepts further interventions with and through music, their effects on symptoms may be far more significant, as illustrated in some of the cases previously cited.

The preceeding case studies serve as examples of ways in which a music therapist can function on a consultation team. They were selected from a multitude of different case histories to reflect the diversity of situations and problems encountered.

This diversity provides an exciting challenge but at the same time can be very stressful. It requires extreme flexibility in often ambiguous circumstances. A music therapist is usually the last person a patient or the traditional health care team expects or wants to see in these critical phases of terminal illness where hope clings to advanced medical knowledge, technology and treatments. "How can you even mention or think of music at this time?" is the unspoken question which continually taxes the music therapist's confidence and convictions and may easily diminish initiative and creativity. It is in this setting, however, that the whole spectrum of therapeutic potential inherent in music, channeled and titrated to the magnitude of individual needs of the patient, particularly exposes the unique scope of music therapy for reaching the total person on the physical, emotional, psycho-social and spiritual level.

It is crucial to acknowledge the impact of this environment as well as to identify one's own feelings of reticence, impotence, fear and occasional repulsion at unsightly disfigurement. Otherwise one may easily start to find pretexts for not seeing difficult patients. Close collaboration and openess with one's colleagues on the team provide invaluable mutual support. Occasional joint visits with either the nurse consultant or a physician who supports music therapy help to ease the uncertainties of the therapist, and at the same time indicate to the patient that music is considered part of the hospital's treatment plan.

SELECTION OF PATIENTS

Time considerations permit only for some of the cases followed by the PCS consultation team to be followed by the music therapist. Cases are presented and reviewed at weekly team rounds and refferals made to the music therapist according to the following criteria:

- complex psychosocial problems
- symptoms of suspected psychogenic origin
- extreme anxiety, restlessness or respiratory difficulties
- fear, insomnia
- withdrawal, anger
- isolation due to
  - danger of infection
  - language barriers
  - absence of speech (brain tumors, laryngectomy)
- need for diversion and motivation

Once initial music therapy interventions had proven to be beneficial in the more complex crisis situations (in the experience of the RVH/PCS), it was obvious that the therapist's skills should be primarily used in those cases. It should not be forgotten, however, that patients with less urgent or complex needs may also benefit from music therapy. For these (often long term patients) trained volunteers can extend the work of the music therapist in a tangible way. The role of "music" volunteers will be specifically addressed in a separate chapter.

FREQUENCY OF VISITS / LENGTH OF INVOLVEMENT / HOSPITAL ENVIRONMENT

It is impossible to establish a general or even average rhythm for music therapy sessions in this type of setting. The patient in crisis might need to be seen two or three times a day, others only daily for some time (on rare occasions also during the weekend) and others at less frequent intervals such as once a week or every two weeks. As two of the previous case examples show, involvement can also be for a single session only.

Since the patients, seen on consultation, are primarily cared for by various acute care medical teams, they may be transferred or discharged abruptly or with only short or no notice at all to the music therapist. When the palliative care team is involved in discharge or transfer planning, the therapist can plan accordingly and may continue to follow the patient at home if appropriate.

Given the general hospital setting, the music therapist has to face interruptions by laboratory and x-ray technicians, ward nurses, physicians, or visitors, as well as to function in the sound environment of television, telephones, intercoms and hospital clatter. The creating of an environment conducive to intimate music experiences therefore constitutes another challenge.

TAPED OR "LIVE" MUSIC?

The reader might question the limited use of music performed by the therapist. Since (in the setting from which the cases are presented) few patients are accomodated in private rooms, the strains of live music immediately attract the attention of all patients in the room and invariably that of anyone in the hallway. Occasionally, depending upon the appropriateness of each situation, this is a desirable and positive therapeutic approach. However, as these case histories document, the needs and circumstances of the individual patient have to be carefully considered. Initially, many of the patients seen are very reticent to even begin thinking of music. After initial hesitation they might eventually be willing to listen to things familiar and precious to them. Often the therapist cannot perform the selections in question, i.e. symphonies and orchestral as well as varied instrumental, vocal or choral works.

One advantage of taped music is its availability at any time of the day or night. Another is the access to "privacy" assured by the use of headphones. As later case studies from the Palliative Care Unit will show, the seriously ill patient might only wish music involvement at certain peak moments of his physical well-being. These will occur at various times when the music therapist is not available, when other roommates dislike noise of any sort, or when the particular music is objectionable.

A tape recorder and tapes also allow the patient to be "in charge" of something at times when control at many other levels is ebbing away.

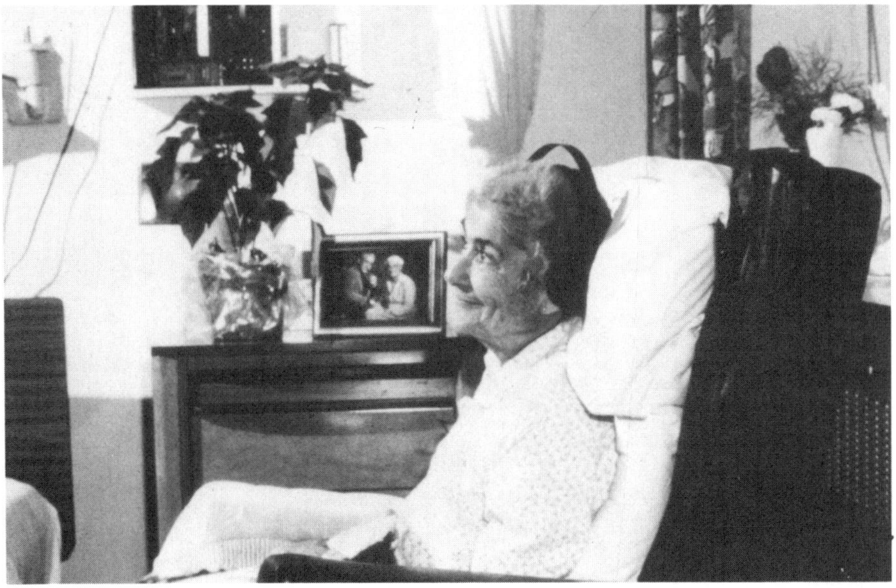

PALLIATIVE CARE INPATIENT UNIT

CASE 1

NOTE AND OBSERVE

- respite care
- patient's habits/routine
- reluctance of patient to leave familiarity of room
- patient's way of relaxation
- paracentesis to music
- discussion of "music world" in hospital setting

Mrs. Anderson was a 72 year old woman with a quiet, gentle air about her and was admitted to the unit for respite care.

The staff learned quickly that Mrs. Anderson was rather particular about routines, not liking change or even suggestions of change. She was fully aware of her diagnosis and prognosis, talking freely about them. She knew the limitations of her strength and conserved her energies carefully for the things she had to or wanted to do (personal hygiene, writing letters, etc.).

Her eyes lit up when I spoke to her about music, especially when she realized she could have her own tape recorder, headphones and a selection of tapes with flute music to listen to when **she** felt like it. My initial offer to play for her was politely turned down because it might disturb others, and she just as kindly turned down the invitation to come to a room where we wouldn't disturb anyone.

I later realized that at home, where her husband's television habits dominated everything, she often longed for her own music world. The fulfillment of this wish at this particular time opened precious new dimensions to her.

I made special flute music tapes or borrowed such from the library and tried to bring her a variety of other selections, but Mrs. Anderson also liked routine as far as music was concerned. She quickly eliminated most things in favour of three flute tapes, of which her favorite was "Songs of the Seashore" played by James Galway. (15)

When she was uncomfortable, she would set herself up with this particular tape, close her eyes and slowly relax. I was therefore not surprised when she asked me if it would be possible to have her music playing when she had to have a paracentesis. The physicians complied readily with her request and the procedure caused her very little discomfort. The physicians talked for days about the serene and peaceful atmosphere that surrounded and united them with the patient during their delicate task. Subsequently, the "Songs of the Seashore" found their way into the record collection of most staff members!

Mrs. Anderson used to look forward to my visits. After a few weeks I was able to play for her and her roomates, which led to some important sharing between them. The patient was now able to receive my playing for her and her friends as a special gift which she treasured, yet accepted on very few occasions.

When she was well enough to go home once again, she refused my offer to take the music home with her, saying that she wouldn't be able to recreate **"her music world,"** which she had grown to love in the hospital.

When she was readmitted, she returned to music for a little while. As her condition deteriorated, however, she listened less and less frequently and accepted just once that I would play for her. "But please don't stop coming to see me," was her request. On my subsequent visits we would often just sit in silence, remembering the musical encounters which we had shared.

CASE 2

NOTE AND OBSERVE

- rapidly progressing disease
- Home Care involvement carries over into PCU situation
- weight of immigrant background and multiple losses
- spouse's denial and difficulties
- sadness, frustration, anxiety, fear displaced into anger at staff
- spiritual impact of music

I knew Mr. Gutmanis from Home Care. He was of Lithuanian origin and on my first visit had readily offered to share his Lithuanian records with me. With the sound of the first few phrases, tears began running down his face, and his wife had instantly turned off the record player! In the following hour all her frustration, anger and bitterness about her husband's illness had spilled forth. They had had to cope with too many losses in their lives already, having fled their home country and lost a son when he was only nine years old. Her husband's illness was the last straw, making her doubt her faith, God and very certainly the medical profession. I sat and listened, trying to share her grief.

Mr. Gutmanis' condition deteriorated very rapidly and made him very weak and drowsy. His wife could not accept these signs of rapidly progressing disease. She found it harder and harder to cope. She had not wanted to hear of music, but since music had provoked her outburst during my first visit and she had found some solace in my sharing and listening, she had trusted me and welcomed several more visits. They had mostly been spent with her since the patient slept much of the day.

When his worsening condition necessitated an admission to the Palliative Care Unit, her distress, anxiety and fatigue manifested themselves in anger and hostility towards the staff. She was convinced her husband did not get adequate care. The confidence she had gained in me occasionally permitted her to relax as I sat with her beside her husband's bed or when I occasionally helped a nurse with his care.

Lung metasteses and pneumonia led to severe congestion and Mrs. Gutmanis became more and more frantic, unable to believe or accept the fast deterioration.

The morning when Mr. Gutmanis slipped into unconsciousness and it had become obvious that he would die soon, she turned to me and said with a quiet, assured voice: "Do you have some Gregorian Chants? He used to love them. We didn't go to church much anymore when they stoped singing Latin Mass and lately I didn't want to face God or religion anyway. But if we could have some of those chants now I think my husband would be in peace."

As the Gregorian Chants filled the room, she cradled her husband's head in her arms and let her tears flow. I stood beside her with my arm around her and felt my own tears running down my cheeks. Two nurses joined us quietly at the bedside. A few minutes later Mr. Gutmanis stopped breathing in a hospital room that, for a while, seemed to have been transformed into a chapel.

When the couple's only daughter arrived a few moments later, (she had gone home a couple of hours earlier only to be called back because of her father's worsening condition), Mrs. Gutmanis instantly turned off the tape recorder. The spell was broken! I then remembered her alllusions to a rift about faith between her daughter and herself.

Mr. Gutmanis was 56 years old. Only seven months had passed since the diagnosis of cancer of the pancreas, metastatic to the liver and descending colon had been made!

CASE 3

NOTE AND OBSERVE

- music as adjunct to physical care
- relaxation induced through non-verbal communication
- bedside care, tuned and adjusted to the rhythm of music and the tension of the patient

While reviewing the night report after Mme Letourneau's admission, the nurses considered best approaches to care for this patient. Her body, from the waist up was very emaciated, but her abdomen and especially her legs were grossly edemetous due to lymphatic obstruction from an ovarian tumor. The patient was also very anxious and tense, which made physical care almost impossible. She just simply wanted to be left alone.

Given this problem, I suggested to the nurse caring for Mme Letourneau that day that we give her a bedbath to music. In order to meet the patient without much ado, I went and assisted her with breakfast and casually wove some questions about music into our conversation. She mentioned that she used to keep her radio tuned to one of the easy listening stations from early morning to night before she got ill. Now, however, she did not feel like listening to music anymore.

"You probably won't believe me, but I used to dance quite well," she suddenly burst out, eyes tearful as she pointed at the bulging silhouette of her legs under the sheets. For a moment I said nothing, but simply put my hand on her arm, sharing her sorrow.

"I can only try to imagine what you must feel, and I understand now that you must dread the idea of even just turning in bed." I then told her about my plan to work with the nurse and use music to help her relax, to which she agreed.

The nurse arranged linens, toilet articles and a clean nightgown within easy reach while I set up a tape recorder with a relaxation tape. The patient smiled faintly when she heard the bird song over the quiet music. (16) "This takes me right to my country cottage," she remarked. We drew the curtain around the bed and began to wash her. The nurse and I synchronized our movements on either side of the bed and adapted them to the ryhthm of the music. Occasionally I encouraged the patient to let her breath flow with this same rhythm and to imagine herself at her country place.

We washed and dried each limb and then paid particular attention to the application of body lotion, which we massaged gently but rhythmically into her skin. By the time we had to turn the patient to her side to wash her back and change the sheets, much of the tension had left her body. The anxious look on her face had vanished and she gave us a grateful smile. When we finished she chuckled: "I feel like a new woman!"

Working slowly with the music had taken extra time but produced the reward of a comfortable patient. Mme Letoureau remained cheerful throughout the day. During the following days the nurses continued to give bedbaths using the same techniques and the patient began once more to enjoy listening to some music.

GROUP SESSION

NOTE AND OBSERVE
- "staging" of group session
- diverse patient population
- music transcends cultural language barriers

The four women in Room 44 were all in their sixties, one of French Canadian, one of Italian, and two of English-Canadian origin. They had all been on the unit for a while, and I previously spent some time with each of them.

Mme Vachon was very quiet and shy, watching closely what was going on in the room and on occasion registering disapprovement on her face. In the next bed was Miss Dolittle, a patient who had a very faithful sister as a daily visitor. This sister had a tendency to make herself at home in the room, always bringing much paraphernalia with her. The pair had obviously lived quite eccentric lives.

Facing this scene was Mrs. Watson who reminded us of a Victorian matron, always very well groomed and often immersed in a book. Her body language and the occasional remark clearly indicated that she preferred not to associate with the other patients.

Signora Mirelli spoke mostly in Italian with only limited French. Her language limitations isolated her from the others, whom she watched rather suspiciously.

I was aware that faith was quite important for each of the patients and when, one morning, the two spinster sisters talked about an old-fashioned portable organ they remembered from their childhood and the hymns they treasured, I seized the opportunity to suggest that we could share some of those right now. Fortunately the other patients were receptive to the idea of music that day, so I moved the piano into the room and played Miss Dolittle's favorite hymn: "Softly and Tenderly Jesus is Calling." The two sisters at first just hummed along but by the second verse began to sing. At that point Mrs. Watson unexpectedly joined in their singing. Momentarily they seemed surprised. The hymn tune had changed the atmosphere and established a link between the different personalities. The words of the hymn united them in common memories and the heritage of faith.

When the song ended Mrs. Watson told Miss Dolittle and her sister she remembered this hymn from her Sunday school days and for a while the three shared memories. They discovered other tunes they all liked, and we sang a few of those.

The two other patients had intently watched the happenings, their faces indicating contentment. At an opportune moment I started to play and sing a hymn tune which is well-known to the French catholic people of Quebec. Timidly and with a smile Mme Vachon joined in the singing, and when we came to the refrain: "Ave, Ave, Ave Maria", Signora Mirelli added her voice to ours. The English speaking patients watched in amazement then hummed for a while and by the third verse quite naturally sang the refrain as well. The ensuing conversation was multilingual. The patients, for the first time, tried to communicate despite language barriers. Each used the few fragments they knew of the foreign languages to convey their memories and associations to the others. At first the conversation centered around hymns, church and faith. Later it turned to home, family, school and travel, and we sang a few folksongs with melodies they all knew: "Greensleeves", "A la claire fontaine", "Santa Lucia" and others. When a nurse joined us, the patients immediately asked for her favorite songs. She liked gospel hymns and negro spirituals, and with her wish for "He's Got the Whole World in His Hands" she led us back to the beginning of our music sharing. With this song we spontaneously expressed the feelings of oneness through faith and the sense of community which we had just experienced.

On subsequent days the incidents of this encounter through hymns and songs remained a very meaningful memory for the four patients. Even though they conversed only slightly more than before, there now was a sense of family between them. They took a new interest in each other's well-being and did not again withdraw into their previous isolation.

MUSIC THERAPY CONSIDERATIONS ON A TERMINAL CARE WARD

The palliative care unit is a place where many patients die. Yet the focus of the care is not on death but rather on life, more particularly on the quality of life for whatever remaining time there may be. The physical environment of the unit has been arranged and decorated to be as much like home as possible. Rooms are bright with colorful curtains and bedspreads. Patients are encouraged to have some of their treasured things around them (pictures, ornaments, souvenirs). Paintings and plants brighten the hallway and there is easy access to a patio. Other special features include a kitchenette, where family members can prepare or heat up patient's favorite foods, a small lounge, where families or staff can quietly retreat when desired and a large lounge designed for recreational and social functions.

Patients and family members often have negative fantasies about the unit and are encouraged, whenever possible, to visit prior to a transfer. Their concerns and fears are carefully considered and transfer plans arranged accordingly. The staff of the palliative care teams will acknowledge with them that the prognosis is uncertain, may indeed be quite short and provide opportunities for patients and families to discuss diagnosis and prognosis if they wish. The degree to which the individual patient or the loved ones acknowledge and integrate the realities of progressive disease varies greatly. It cannot be assumed that patients will want to talk about their impending death. If some degree of denial is playing a protective function for the patient or a person close to him or her, it should be respected. Even in the case of families who have bravely faced terminal illness for some time, the reality of transfer to the unit may cause an unexpected tumult of feelings which occasionally will be manifested in hostility, anger or utter despair.

The music therapist finds him or herself in the midst of these happenings and has to use good judgement in choosing appropriate moments and settings for music involvement. If patients are known to the therapist from home care or consultation, it will be easier to adapt approaches to a terminal admission. The patient (or family members) might not want to be even reminded of music at this particular time, or the complexity of symptoms may completely monopolize the patient's attention. The fact that the music therapist has shared some meaningful moments through music before admission can make him or her, in some cases, a trusted resource person for the patient or the family. The therapist's time, in such situations, is often spent in "being there" to listen, reminisce or to establish a link between the homecare or consultation team and the unit staff.

Mrs. Gutmanis (whom we considered earlier) would probably have met the therapist with the same hostility she showed towards other staff members had she not known her from previous encounters. At the same time the therapist was reticent to touch the subject of music in the crisis situation because this woman had not been able to tolerate the impact of music in less stressful circumstances. Without the association of that previous experience and the therapist's presence, however, Mrs. Gutmanis would probably never have thought of Gregorian Chants at the moment of her husband's death.

Before meeting a newly admitted patient in the palliative care unit, it is essential for the music therapist to familiarize herself with the case history, in particular with psychosocial and symptom problems. Approximately 80% of Palliative Care Unit admissions are terminal admissions, usually necessitated by complex physical symptoms, nursing needs or manifold psychosocial issues. Case history forms include mention of leisure time activities and often provide an opening for inquiries about previous music interests. The majority of people associate music with happy, social occasions, and even its mention in the final stages of illness may be perceived out of place by patients or family. The music therapist therefore is not necessarily involved with all patients on the unit, and may serve only as a consultant to the nurse who is primarily charged with that individual's case.

CULTURAL ISSUES

The multiple ethnic background of patients followed by the PCS demands that cultural perspectives regarding death and dying need also be considered before thinking of or suggesting the use of music. For example, a man from Pakistan stated, interpreted through his son, that he was waiting to meet his God and wanted to spend the time in prayer; music would stand between him and God. At another time, a Greek family was appalled at the thought of music when their mother was dying.

In certain circumstances music **can** play an important role in transcending language and cultural barriers. The presence of music from their homeland has brought many immigrant patients a connection with tradtions and associations from the past. Such patients often long particularly for their native country and family as they face death. Music may help them trace back to their roots, and to feel less isolated and alone in a foreign land.

CONTINUED LIVING IN THE FACE OF DYING

Palliative Care focuses on the quality of life at any stage of terminal illness. Paramount attention is given to the best possible medical symptom control and total person care. The primary goal of this kind of care, respecting the universal wish for independence, is to allow the individual to keep as much control in decision making as possible, for as long as possible.

The home-like atmosphere of the unit to some extent encourages the patient to continue normal living habits. But when weakness increases, bringing decreased mobility, we particularly need to nurture motivation to continue participation in life's activities. Tape recorders and radios naturally substitute for similar equipment which was left at home. Staff have to assure their accessability on night and bedside tables, and the patient is encouraged to be in charge if at all possible. The mobile patient can personally select tapes from the cassette library at any time of the day or night. A "trip" to choose cassettes can be a goal for the individual who needs to be mobilized or the wheelchair-bound person.

For some families, who always considered music as an integral part of their lives, the mobile stereo unit transforms the hospital room into home. The wife of a brain tumor patient spent many days playing records of dance music and songs to her husband, who no longer could communicate, thus continuing to share her memories and tell him through the songs about her love and the love they shared. In this manner she could continue to care in a tangible way at a time when her helplessness seemed overwhelming.

As the patient nears death, we have to be sensitive to the possible need for reflection, detatchment and gradual withdrawal. Music might be the first or the last thing the patient ceases to take interest in. When cassettes remain untouched they should not be immediately removed since the patient might interpret such action as the caregiver's giving up.

If the music therapist can create an environment where music is available, accessable and considered an important dimension of care, the patients will choose that from which they draw most benefit. Mrs. Anderson knew best when she needed the comfort of music and other patients did likewise.

Words often fail to express the difficulties and struggles in the transition of the dying patient. The unique non-verbal qualities of music often reach deeper than anything else. The full extent of the impact of such communication between an individual and music remains as much of a mystery as the process of dying. Interpretations are inadequate and attempts at verbalization may destroy the magic connection music provided.

> John, a 38 year old university professor, immobilzed by an aggresive spinal tumor, often listened to music. His interactions with the therapist were friendly. Yet, as with other staff members, he evaded any conversation touching on the seriousness of his condition. He spoke about music in strictly intellectual terms, never alluding to any emotional or affective qualities. He loved the music of Bach, Mozart and the song cycles of Schubert. The therapist provided the tapes he asked for and respected his unspoken wish to talk only about composers, composition and musical structure. His choices and his behavior indicated that he drew comfort and deep satisfaction from the music. One day he asked for Mozart's

Requiem. The therapist, aware that the composer wrote it on his deathbed at the age of thirty five, took the risk to comment on the apparent parallel. John immediately withdrew, saying it was really unimportant that he hear that music.

The therapist had intruded on the intimate communication between a person and his music. John felt exposed and chose to retreat.

SYMPTOM CONTROL

Symptom control in Palliative Care Unit patients remains an important challenge for the staff team. The music therapist can add her skills to those of nurses and physicians and use approaches as described in the consultation case stories.

While a patient plagued by frequent vomiting does not likely want to hear of music, the latter occasionally can provide enough distraction to re-focus the person's attention and thus help relax aggravated muscular wretching reflexes.

Causes of insomnia are not always definable and have undercurrents of anxiety, fear or unexplainable restlessness. Here, music can be a presence, a lullaby, a diversion that helps to shorten long wakeful nights or bring unexpected sleep. Relaxation tapes, the patient's favorite pieces, easy listening popular music or environmental sounds have proven helpful in such circumstances.

Pain control in the case of a young surgeon deeply puzzled physician and nurses. The patient could not sleep and the music therapist was asked if she could help.

She met the patient and talked to him about music, stressing its non-verbal qualities and the possibilities of its physiological impact on the body. He had not touched music (piano or records) for quite some time, preoccupied by the diagnosis and pain problems, and at first seemed unprepared to accept music as a treatment modality. The therapist left him a tape recorder, tapes and headphones, allowing him the choice of using or not using these things. In the selection of tapes she included an "Environment Tape" (17) with the sounds of the ocean and the rain in a pine forest. She drew his attention to these.

Later in the day the patient decided to listen to the ocean waves, fell asleep and subsequently spent a restful night. Adequate sleep helped to improve pain control and on his discharge he left a note on the music therapist's desk: "A sincere thank you for helping me with your relaxation tapes and suggestions."

GROUP SESSIONS

Much of the music therapist's work on the in-patient ward needs to be done on an individual basis. Group sessions are most appropriate and effective if they can evolve naturally in a given situation, as illustrated in the case example. Given the relatively small patient population on the Palliative Care Unit; the variety of ethnic, social, intellectual and religious backgrounds, the diversity in ages and the complexity of symptom problems, there were few opportunities for group sessions. A larger, more ethnically homogeneous patient pool might facilitate more frequent group interaction.

In general, experience has shown many patients very reticent to leave their room to attend group events. Their physical status often allows them only short periods of concentration or relative well-being, and by the time the staff has gathered the last of a handful of patients in the lounge the first one might likely want to return to his room.

The sound of music carries from room to room, another fact that necessitates careful observation since it can be valuable or disturbing depending on the individual situations.

Each death on the unit leaves it's mark on fellow patients and staff, and planned music events often have to be postponed either because they are inappropriate when death occurs or because there needs to be time for sadness and grieving. Advance planning becomes almost impossible for the music therapist. The relatives of patients are frequently present and should be drawn into music therapy if possible. At the same time a relative might object to music while the patient likes it. This issue needs to be diplomatically addressed.

With all this in mind it becomes evident that the administering of music in all situations of terminal care has to be as carefully titrated as the administering of medication. At the same time, music touches dimensions of personhood and suffering that cannot be reached by medication or good nursing care.

The following case study, written by a physican, further illustrates this phenomenon:

> As a keen music lover, I have since childhood experienced and "lived" the power of music. In the large university teaching hospital in which I work, music therapy was unheard of, except in some references to rather dilettante experiences on psychiatric wards, until a music therapist joined the staff of the Palliative Care Service.
>
> Music therapy, like music itself, can hardly be defined, but is, like fresh air on your cheek, easliy felt and yet invisible. Through the able mind and heart of our music therapist, I have witnessed innumerable times the effects not only of music 'per se' (it would be too easy - and useless I am sure - to install speakers in each room as in a restaurant) but especially of **music therapy**, that is of music brought to the patients or patients brought to the music in a way **meaningful to them.** One patient stands out in my memory as an example of the extraordinary power of music which enters hearts often closed to everything and everybody else.
>
> Mr. Simpson, aged 51, was dying of widespread cancer of the prostate which had given him very painful bone lesions and immobilized him with semi-paralized legs.

He probably had never been seen crying since childhood. Six foot three, 225 lbs of muscle, he had been a boxer for many years. Then he "retired" as a barman in a tavern where, as might be expected, his stature, strength and previous career qualified him to handle every "roughneck" who made too much noise. He was soft-spoken, kind and surprisingly gentle-mannered. With his strength, he did not need to be rough.

I first met him on consultation. He lay on his back, with his arms crossed over his face. When I said "Hello", he swiftly wiped a tear from his eyes as he uncovered his face.

"You are discouraged," I said. "It's not that. It's the pain." I sensed that he wanted me to believe he never felt discouraged. His wife, a tiny woman weighing less than 100 lbs and measuring less than five feet, later confirmed that he had always acted like the tough guy who never hurt, had always been kind and gentle to her, but had never in 25 years of marriage communicated anything about feelings, certainly not about his own.

I met the patient several times. Once his pain was really under control he became friendly and more open with me. However, he never discussed any topic where personal feelings might have surfaced.

His improved condition allowed him to be discharged again for several months. He was readmitted with a suddenly collapsed spinal column, his legs shaking uncontrollably because of pinched nerves, and he had nearly lost all muscle strength. He also suffered excruciating lower back pain.

His face was like those one imagines in horror movies. He was panic-stricken, breathing rapidly and moaning unintelligibile words. I think "disaster" had suddenly entered his mind. The strong man he no longer was could not protect the young boy, never yet grown-up in him. He was facing for the first time the horrible killer called **cancer.**

The nurses could neither comfort him nor calm him. He was agitated, clinging to the raised bedsides and shaking them. He didn't seem to hear any word spoken to him and gave the impression of a wild, wounded animal. I left the room for a moment to discuss his management with the nurse in charge at the nursing station. When I returned, only a few minutes later, Mr. Simpson was quietly leaning against the pillows of the raised head of the bed. Tears ran down his cheeks and he didn't make a move to hide them. Incredible!

He looked at me and smiled faintly. We didn't speak but it seemed to me that through these tears he shed all the ones he had supressed for years and for the first time in his life he experienced and enjoyed the deep, existential soothing released in crying. At the same time he accepted the presence of a friend or mate in the spirit of true friendship, allowing his real inner-self to be exposed.

A nurse had had the good judgement to treat the irrationality of sorrow with the irrationality of beauty. She had simply brought and turned on a relaxation tape, especially prepared by our music therapist.

Where all human and medical efforts at soothing the despair and agitation failed, the trancendental, universal and eternal beauty of music had reached into this man's heart; a man afraid and too deeply hidden, even to himself, unreachable either by the spoken word or by the human touch of nursing.

Marcel Boisvert M.D.

Words can never reach far enough into music to touch her essence. However, with trying, our words will become more musical, our respect and wonder more absorbing, our understanding of music and ourselves deeper.

C. BEREZNAK KENNY

BEREAVEMENT FOLLOW-UP

BEREAVEMENT FOLLOW-UP

Music was a thread running through Gerard's life which turned into a lifeline for his wife Lise. Music therapy facilitated this transformation, and the flute music during the memorial service marked an important pivotal point in this process. For the therapist, this event represented a significant moment of closure in which she could offer the gift of music whose meaning and power had penetrated to the depth of human experience in the face of death. For Lise this music became the link from the past into the future, a bridge over which she could travel back and forth whenever she needed to in the months that followed.

Obviously there are only some instances where the music therapist actually participates in the funeral service. Families, on occasion, will ask about music for the memorial service of a loved one or more frequently inquire if they could borrow a tape, which had been particularly meaningful to the patient during the last weeks or days of his life. Weeks or months later, when the bereaved person is ready for some closure, he or she will send it or bring it back, eager to review the events before death once more and at the same time ready to relate elements of the healing process discovered through music.

Examples like the following show that music can provide invaluable comfort in the grieving process, an area of music therapy inadequately explored to date.

Frank was in the hospital for six months before he died. During this time pain control proved a continued challenge to the team of physicians. Tumor erosion at the bottom of the spine necessitated involved and complicated nursing care. Frank had been a public relations manager of a large corporation and insisted on relating to the hospital staff as if they were part of the office staff, politely but at a distance. Everyone involved in the care faced feelings of inadequacies as the symptoms persisted and recurred each time one hoped that a new treatment or medication had taken effect.

Early in his admission music had helped to diminish pain through relaxation but as time went on and pain persisted Frank wasn't interested in listening to music, taped or live. The music therapist continued to visit him once or twice a week and at one point was able to help him tape part of an article he had wanted to write. Some tapes were always left at his bedside. On the whole, however, as the months slowly went by, the therapist felt inadequate and helpless, knowing that music could not improve the patient's situation.

Frank's wife could only visit in the evenings and the therapist only met her once. On that occasion the woman seemed tired and rather withdrawn.

When Frank died, his personal tape recorder was mistakenly put away with the hospital equipment and as soon as the therapist discovered the error she contacted his wife. In the conversation Mrs. E. mentioned that she had occasionally used Frank's tapes in the evenings while sitting at his bedside when he was asleep, and had found them of great help. She asked for details about the "bird" tape (16) and when the therapist sent her the tape recorder she included that tape as a token gift.

A month later she received a note in which the widow related how she had found comfort and rest at their country cottage where the music had helped her re-live moments of her husband's illness, and yet had led her to find new strength and meaning in the beauty of ''real'' nature which surrounded her there.

MUSIC THERAPY VOLUNTEERS

MUSIC THERAPY VOLUNTEERS

The essence of good palliative/hospice care is attention to detail; comprehensive review of symptoms and attention to all the small individual needs that distinguish impersonal "sufficing" care from personal "exceptional" care. Since no professional team will ever have the time to fulfill this mandate adequately, volunteers complement the multidisciplinary team in a very tangible way. They are available to nurses and staff whenever help is needed and provide support and campanionship to patients and their families. The RVH Palliative Care Service relies on the assistance of many volunteers on the unit, on consultation and home care as well as in the bereavement follow-up program.

Once a music therapist's work load increases, help from volunteers is essential to the program and such help may be given in the following areas:

- monitoring and maintenance of audio equipment
- tape library — record search, cataloguing, taping
- patient follow-up — exchanging tapes, nurturing of music interest
- resources — varied cultural backgrounds, instrumental skills

When the need for more resources to assist the music therapist became evident in the RVH/PCS, the first step taken was to present the problem to the group of volunteers already working actively on the PCS. Although several were interested in adding a music focus to their skills, it soon became evident that an effective team required volunteers who saw this as the major focus of their work.

During this trial and error period a couple of musicians, both with a keen interest in and some workshop experience with music therapy, applied as volunteers to the Palliative Care Service. They were interviewed and screened by the volunteer coordinator and the music therapist, accepted and subsequently worked for the accustomed orientation period on the Palliative Care Unit to familiarize themselves with the concept of palliative care and the role of the volunteer on the multidisciplinary team. Following this introduction time, their services were available to the music therapist who now could organize her work with the help of five volunteers, the two musicians, and three from the original group of experienced volunteers. One volunteer would be available for about four hours each day.

With this help it was possible to explore music needs and wishes with an extended group of patients, especially some of the long term cases where symptoms were less acute, and a nurturing of motivation for continued creative living was essential.

Variety in the musical and cultural background of this team of music volunteers provided a valuable addition to the music therapist's skills. Josee had grown up with the musical traditions of Quebec, was very much at home with the songs and custom of this culture and therefore had a special way of relating to a patient with the same roots. Naomi became the music therapist's "Jewish advisor" in helping her to define the role of particular pieces in the Jewish traditions, and often most effectively sharing music with a very ill person of the Jewish faith. Valerie, a violinist and Mary, a pianist, on occasion played for patients alone or in duet with the therapist. Therese, a very experienced volunteer on the Palliative Care Unit, integrated her love for music in her work at the bedside, and would readily solicit some music sharing from a patient while being involved in his physical care.

The music therapist coordinated the music interactions with patients. Information was communicated between team members through a volunteer book in the therapist's office. The volunteers helped with the monitoring of equipment, the search for musical materials and the taping whenever time permitted. An additional volunteer, recruited from the city's volunteer service, spent one day a week on the continued upkeep of the tape library.

The invaluable potential benefits of a music therapy volunteer team will only be realized if sufficient attention is paid to selection, training and supervision of such volunteers.

Individuals have to be willing to commit themselves over an extended period of time and be prepared to function in collaboration with the therapist and other team members. They do not necessarily have to be musicians but music should have important meaning for them. An extended training period as a general volunteer is important even for the person who intends to work only with the music therapist. Good listening and observation skills, sensitivity in difficult interpersonal encounters and ease at the bedside are essential prerequisites for a music volunteer. These are developed during the orientation to patient care. Later it is the music therapist's responsibility to channel musical talents to particular patient's needs and to set limits as to appropriate involvement.

Volunteers can never substitute for a skilled music therapist! Music is a powerful medium, and a person is defenceless against its impact on the emotions. The terminally ill person already faces much emotional upheaval. Music can comfort, reach and bring pleasure, but it may also touch hidden pains, memories and suffering which will have to be worked through and possibly resolved to assure healing of a person's inner being. A music therapist is trained to facilitate such a process and integrate its outcome into the general treatment plan of the patient. This kind of therapeutic intervention lies beyond the mandate of a volunteer.

TEAM WORK

TEAM WORK

A music therapist could not function in the ways described in this book unless he or she were part of a mutildisciplinary team, sharing in the complex care of the terminally ill person. It is hoped that the case examples document some aspects of this inegrated team approach in the clinical reality.

In my experience, it has been beneficial to be present at early morning report with nurses at least after the weekend or after prolonged periods of absence from the Palliative Care ward. Many details regarding the patient, his family, nursing and medication issues are passed on in such a report and provide necessary orientation. The therapist together with the nurse can set priorities for the day's activities.

The nurse is readily accepted at the bedside whereas the music therapist may be perceived as an intruder. A nurse, sensitive to music and its role and place in people's lives, can discover the **"music person"*** in her patient just as the therapist would as long as she is familiar with this concept. The nurse and the patient may casually exchange their perceptions about music while a bed bath is given; the patient doesn't feel interviewed and attention may very naturally shift from hospital and illness to memories and life issues. The idea of music as a treatment modality can then later be more easily introduced. Given the reticence towards music involvement often encountered, such an introduction frequently facilitates later interactions. The involvement of the music therapist in the physical care of a patient is an unfamiliar concept in hospital or music therapy circles. The nursing dependency rating (measure of nursing requirements in patient care) is higher on the Palliative Care Unit than in all other wards of the general hospital except in the cardiac unit (18), and the physical care of a patient may take up several hours during the course of a day. In this context, physical care is the essence of "comfort care". **When we consider the body of the care giver as an instrument which requires careful tuning, we maximize the effects of our interactions through body language and touch.**

This concept evolved from the therapist's interventions in crisis situations. Through appropriate body language, reassurance by means of touch and the use of rhythm in movement and breathing, the patient may be guided towards relaxation **without** verbal communication before music can positively reach the person's ear and deepen or extend the relaxation effect.* In the same manner, the body language of the care giver influences the patient. The nurse/therapist teamwork as described in Mme Letourneau's case, involved the combination of nursing skills with music, music therapy and movement skills and proved to be very effective. Such techniques, once introduced, can later be applied by the nurses alone.

Music experience, among other things, is influenced by the environment in which it is perceived or lived. The hospital environment is not naturally conducive to such ventures. The music therapist therefore needs the support and sensitivity of other staff members if patients are to benefit from music. At the same time he/she should realize that for many years traditional health care philosophy has not considered music as a treatment modality and health care professionals will need time to develop such perspectives.

In the case of the Palliative Care Service, the music therapist gave several workshops for members of the multidisciplinary team. In this way nurses, physicians, volunteers, chaplain, social worker and physiotherapist could explore dimensions of non-verbal communication through instruments or movement; projective tech-

* see p. 35

* see p. 30

niques through drawing and collages as well as aspects of environment; therapeutic touch and massage. These experiences greatly increased the individual awareness of all team members, which translated into increased sensitivity towards music's potential in the work with patients.

Nurses who had participated in a workshop or observed the music therapist with patients would thus begin to think more readily of using a relaxation tape for a restless or anxious patient during the night rather than immediately opt for an increase in medication. Likewise such nurses would draw the attention of the music therapist to a particular patient's problems or needs. This often led to joint planning of a "music approach" which later would be implemented by the nurse or other care giver.

It is inevitable that such interaction leads to a blurring of traditional role definitions, and unless team members continually work on the nurturing of trust relationships, feelings of threat about one's own role may develop easily.

Should the music therapist voice concerns about nursing or social work issues? Should the nurse or the chaplain establish a music relationship with a patient without consulting the music therapist? The complexity of whole person care in terminal illness may at times require that one person, to whom the patient seems to relate easily, will have to assume a leading role in the coordination and administration of the care. This role may fall on any member of the team, who in turn will have to respond to concerns about medical, nursing, spiritual, social or other issues, thus overstepping established role territory.

While this team concept most certainly benefits the patient, it is often stress-inducing for a group of very diverse professionals who continually have to face crises, death and grief in situations where role expectations and job descriptions are liable to be inadequately defined. Thus, staff stress (19) is an inevitable issue for the multidisciplinary team involved in terminal care, and in many palliative/hospice care settings special meetings are scheduled solely for staff support.

The music therapist always encounters incomplete understanding of his/her role, and of the potential of music therapeutic intervention, and must have the opportunity of being included in team meetings on patient or staff stress related themes. This commitment should be considered in establishing a time schedule for the position of a music therapist in the hospice setting.

The input of the music therapist can open new horizons on music therapy as an art form or as a key to personal growth for other staff members. In fact, the Palliative Care Service staff at the R.V.H. occasionally requested music involvement for themselves. In sharing significant personal music preferences, team members drew closer to each other's "music person" and their emotional language. Informal sing-a-longs nurtured a community spirit and frequently led to singing for patients. Individuals would seek out the music therapist to extend and explore their own music world or to share their discoveries.

A seed is sown for the integration of the healing process through music into the traditional medical model of care when the care givers can experience the combination of personal music involvement and witness music therapeutic work with patients.

Wall Unit for Individual Tape Decks

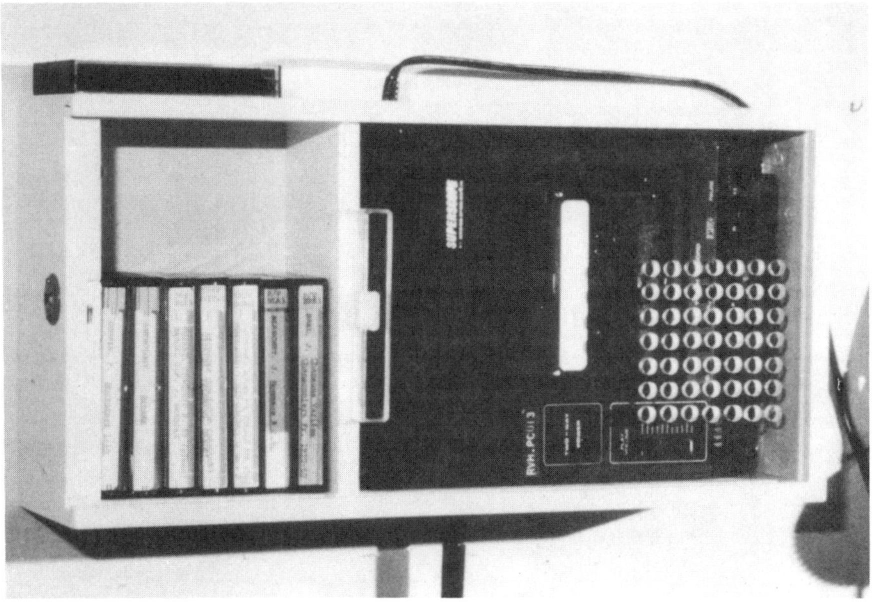

EQUIPMENT • CASSETTE LIBRARY • INSTRUMENTS

EQUIPMENT • CASSETTE LIBRARY • INSTRUMENTS

A music therapist who is asked to set up a program in a palliative/hospice care setting will sooner or later have to address issues of audio equipment, taped materials and musical instruments. The observations and suggestions that will be presented here reflect personal experience over a five year period in a palliative care setting.

The availability of small tape recorders for bedside use widens, without a doubt, the scope of music therapeutic intervention, and in the settings documented in this manual, these machines (20) have proven to be the most frequently used music equipment. By now, a specially designed wall unit, where the tape recorders, a few tapes and headphones can be stored, is installed beside each bed on the Palliative Care Unit.

This setup has the following advantages:

- equipment is easily accessible without cluttering the already often cramped bedside table
- the design of the unit allows for the tape recorder to be easily removed in order to set it up within the patient's reach
- the equipment is immediately at hand and ready to function, particularly important in crisis situations
- the wall unit can easily be locked to prevent theft of the equipment.

If such a setup is not available, equipment will need to be carefully monitored to prevent loss and theft, especially in the larger hospital setting. Identification numbers can be engraved into the plastic or metal casings for inventory purposes.

Sound quality should primarily determine the choice of small tape recorders. Since these machines will be used by many different people, the quality of material and the construction is of importance as well (push buttons have to withstand continued wear). The amount of pressure needed to depress buttons also deserves attention, since patients are often very weak. On/off markings might have to be identified with additional color dots on all visible surfaces of the pushbutton to give easy visual cues.

Headphones have to be very light, soft and adjustable. They will at times be worn over scarves or hats which hide the loss of hair and patients are generally very sensitive to even the slightest pressure on their heads. Headphones can also be simply laid beside the person's head or replaced by a pillow speaker. (Small plastic speaker disc, which can be put under or on top of the pillow). The sound quality of the latter is unfortunately rather poor.

Ideally a mobile stereo unit (a cabinet on rollers with record-player, tapedeck, speakers and room for some records) should complement the audio equipment. It will facilitate the following:

- patient's records can be played as soon as they are brought in and immediately taped for continued bedside use
- individual selections are more easily identified on records than on tapes
- the sound quality of such equipment is more suitable for use in a larger room (lounge or occasionally multiple bedroom)

A cassette tape library takes time to acquire and should mainly grow from the music which is meaningful to patients. Since monitoring of tapes is essential, and they will have to be accessible to patients, families and staff, a basic library system has to be considered. The tapes of the Palliative Care Service library are color-coded for easy overall identification (a color label for each of the following music sections: classical, light classical, popular, ethnic, religious, poetry, special effects i.e. environment, relaxation). Tapes are further identified with titles and numbers and a reference catalogue facilitates the search for a particular item. Any tape or tape recorder taken to patients on homecare and consultation is signed out either by the music therapist, a staff-member or a volunteer.

It is inevitable that some tapes will be lost or occasionally damaged if the tape library is accessible to so many different people, but a more rigid system would not allow staff to respond to particular music needs at any time of the day or the night.

In the RVH/Palliative Care Service the advantages of the readily available tape library, located centrally on the Palliative Care Unit, override by far any disadvantages.

As stated earlier, we frequently encounter reticence to active music involvement in the terminally ill patient; a fact that can partially be attributed to decreased physical strength and well-being. Occasionally however, the use of small instruments can provide meaningful stimulation and music encounter.

- a young man, immobilized with paralyzed legs from tumor pressure, whose native island was Barbados, immensely enjoyed playing small bongo drums to the sounds and songs of Harry Belafonte. His extraordinary drumming skills earned him much praise from fellow patients and staff
- a ninety year old gentleman who, years ago, had played the violin, renewed his interest in playing on a small bow harp (21)
- a man, totally frustrated by his confinement to bed and the loss of his voice through a tracheotomy, found a new way to expression on a kalimba which he chose from a selection of small ethnic instruments
- a Choroi harp (22) tuned pentatonically to a wooden flute (copy of a renaissance instrument) allowed patients without previous musical experiences to improvise with the therapist

Such instruments are small, do not require much physical exertion and can be played in bed. Their simplicity easily overrides the patient's concerns about musical inability; yet, through their sound quality, they readily awake curiosity and interest.

MONITORING OF AUDIO EQUIPMENT AND TAPES

DATE OUT	TAPE RECORDER NUMBER	TAPE NUMBERS	PATIENTS	WHERE	DATE IN
4.22.84	# 21	IGN-1, MOZ-11, MOZ-2, HAY-1, MOU-1, MUS. FOR ZEN MEDITATION	MS. LEBLANC	10 W	5.18.82
4.29.82	# 12	SOU-1, MEL-1, MOZ-3	MR. GORDOZA	10 M	5.11.82
4.29.82	# 15	BEE-9, BAC-10, BAC-8, BAC-7, HAY-3	MS. WALSH	WP Rm 508	5.10.82
5. 6.82	# 23	FID-1, MAD-1, LAS-2, SOU-1	MRS. WARIENKO	WP/4E	5.27.82
5. 8.82	uses own	VIV-3, MOU-2, RAC-1	MRS. ELEMO	MNI/3 S Rm 68	5.17.82
5.11.82 5.18.82	# 18	MOR-1, MIL-1, EVA-2, FIE-1, GYP-2, LAS-3	MRS. CROLL	R 2	5.27.82
5.19.82	# 29	ALB-2, BAC-4, REL-4, JAP-2	MR. ASCHER	R 3	5.25.82
5.21.82	# 21	REL-3, LIG-5, MOU-2, LAS-3, MOZ-2	MME. PICKER	WP/8 E	5.25.82
5.24.82	# 28	SIN-3, BEL-1, REL-2	MRS. HENDERSON	6 M Rm 16	5.26.82

Small Instruments of Ethnic Origin

''Choroi'' Harp

PART TWO

A CHALLENGING JOURNEY
PERSPECTIVES FOR THE MUSIC THERAPIST

I believe that helping a person to move toward full humanness proceeds inevitably via awareness of one's identity.

A.H. Maslow

The preceding case histories and considerations are unavoidably tinged with elements of my personal perceptions, background, education, music therapy training and philosophical attitudes. While I perceive the identity of the music therapist as a key issue in any therapeutic intervention, I consider it indispensable to carefully elucidate the therapist's cognition of his or her very personal feelings, fears, doubts and struggles in the face of work with the terminally ill.

In working with dying patients one is inevitably confronted by one's own finiteness and existential framework of thought and emotion. At the same time one brings one's own professional bias and expectations to a setting where rational thinking and expectancy is constantly challenged by complex, ever-changing physical care components intermingled with psychological, psychosocial, emotional and metaphysical considerations which are often only partially definable on a rational level. Given the presence of such dichotomies and the reality that the role of a music therapist is relatively unknown in a medical setting, the job mandate of the latter is probably best described as "foggy", and requires continual redefinition.

I was fortunate enough to be given a two month period as a trainee on the Palliative Care Unit before I had to begin functioning as a music therapist and would recommend such an introduction to any colleague who accepts a music therapy position in a hospice setting. Extensive reading of the death and dying literature had certainly prepared me only partially for the realities of terminal care. As I worked with the nurses, I learned to face and comprehend the impact of physical symptoms (tumor sights, decubitus ulcers, vomiting, intractible pain, congestion, etc.) and to observe, even question my own reactions. I also acquired some nursing skills which later proved invaluable when with a patient who needed assistance. Those weeks allowed me to consider possible music therapy approaches without the immediate pressure of having to implement them and to tune into the life and experiences of staff and patients on the ward.

At the same time patients became my teachers. I remember the lady who, probably without knowing it, taught me the importance of simply being present even in the face of helplessness, as I assisted her through hours of intermittent vomiting that could not be controlled. While innumerable questions about the meaning of illness and life as well as doubts about the medical and nursing interventions went through my mind and I felt totally inadequate in this overwhelming situation, she quietly reassured me that my presence and whatever assistance I gave her meant a lot and was sufficient.

During this initial training period I began to focus closely on two seemingly contradictory goals of terminal care: helping to live in order to facilitate dying. Where should the emphasis of music therapy be directed? My previous music therapy experiences in training and later in both a psychiatric hospital and an institution for retarded children had taught me to focus on living; communication, expression, socialization, motivation, participation. Now, with the realities of pain, sadness, withdrawal, weakness and progressive disease confronting me constantly, these goals needed to be redefined and carefully integrated in a context where living, on the one hand was limited by time yet, on the other, unlimited in scope for human growth magnified in the face of death.

Contrary to my expectations, gleaned from literature and hearsay, few patients talked openly and easily about their illness and impending death, yet concern and worry about such reality was ever present, hidden behind different facades. How was I to introduce a music therapy that could reach behind and beyond such barriers?

Today, five years later, I know that a music therapist who really wants to meet terminally ill patients where they are and not where the therapist thinks they should be, will continually have to struggle to adapt goals and approaches between two poles — living and dying. It is easier to focus one's therapeutic intervention on living, but only if one is sensitive and open to the reality of dying will one be able to nurture and witness the transition and shift of perspectives. In concrete terms this means that the therapist has to allow patients to choose their personal way of dealing with the illness. At the same time he or she has to be prepared to suggest therapeutic intervention through music which permits the transition period between life and death to come into focus and to be prepared to accompany the patient through this transition.

MUSIC THERAPY — By Whose Consent?

In the psychiatric and institutional settings in which I had previously worked, patients had usually been assigned to music therapy by a physician or by team decision. Little or no option about whether of not to attend sessions was left to the individuals. Naturally they could refuse participation once on the spot, but I always encountered objection from other health professionals when I defended the patient's right to such refusal rather than agreeing to label the behavior as inappropriate!

Did the patient's mental impairment allow us to decide for the individual (especially in areas of music involvement) when there was still little conclusive evidence available as to the depth of emotional impact of music? What was acceptable behavior in such circumstances anyway? Despite the realization that answers to such controversial questions will always lie in gray areas, I have always felt that music therapists did not address these issues adequately. In our zealous efforts to convince others about the many benefits of music, we generally ignore to caution against the misuse of this powerful tool to manipulate and invade the feelings and emotions of others!

The palliative care situation brought these disquieting reflections abruptly into renewed focus. Here the emphasis **was** on meeting the patients on their own terms and to include them and their loved ones in the decision making process around the care. The implication of informed consent, which Weisman defines as "...an obligation which guarantees the perogative to choose or refuse..." (23), remained a continual source of stress and questioning even for the most motivated health care team who believed sincerely in a whole person approach and the patient's choices in decision making. We were inevitably caught between learned professional patterns and habits, the overwhelming complexities of patient's needs and struggles, and individual perceptions and beliefs concerning the new style of dying, pungently described by Phillippe Aries:

> "We now have a new 'style of dying' or rather 'an acceptable style of living while dying', 'an acceptable style of facing death'. The emphasis is on **acceptable.** What is important is that one die in a manner that can be accepted and tolerated by the survivor." (24)

While this might be a rather strong statement about the death and dying concepts which evolved in recent years, it nevertheless underlines a trend with which palliative/hospice care teams struggle. The reader might want to turn to the literature on death, dying and hospice care for further reflections on the subject.

These contemplations are significant in the context of this book in so far as they directly influence the approach in music therapy with the terminally ill person. We should not presume that music will or should reach these patients nor simply impose live or piped in music on them for reasons such as "It will cheer them up,"

"Things are so gloomy and quiet around here," "It's important to keep on living." Music, and its therapeutic application, is ONE other dimension we can offer in palliative care. But it has to be proposed with utmost sensitivity and respect for the vulnerability of the seriously ill person who has to be given the option of refusing music intervention.

As I began to define my role as a music therapist on the Palliative Care Unit, the crystallization of this attitude was achieved through much soul searching. I sensed the expectations of the staff to see me in action, playing music for and with patients and demonstrating the effects of such interventions. I brought with me the expectations of myself as an effective therapist in other settings and the newly gained perceptions of my time as a trainee. But as I faced the first interventions with patients, I quickly realized that **only when I forgot about expectations, dared to be patient and to leave choices and initiatives to the individual, did music become an effective treatment mode in this kind of care.** At the same time it was up to me to find ways of introducing to patients the music perspectives which were acceptable to **them** and which would nurture therapeutic objectives.

I hope the various case studies reflect the essence of this attitude and approach. What they only allude to, however, is the continued uncertainty and frequent doubts about the role and effectiveness, imagined and real, that the therapist lives with in the terminal care setting, where the relentless evolution of disease perpetually erodes any sense of control. This context stretches the therapist's capacity for flexibility to the limits.

RISKS AND LIMITS

In the light of the preceeding paragraphs let us take another look at the palliative care philosophy and then focus once again on the role of music therapy in that perspective.

To palliate is defined as to reduce the violence of; abate. In the palliative care/hospice setting, it means the reduction or abatement of pain and other troubling symptoms by appropriate coordination of all elements of care needed to achieve relief from distress. The emphasis is on **total care.** Patients are seen as persons rather than a disease process and are considered in their social context with their extended family as a unit of care. In recognizing that understanding the needs of the total person requires time and the caregiver's undivided attention, the staff/patient relationship takes on significant proportions. Only as the patient begins to trust in the genuine interest of the caregiver, will he or she be able to drop some defenses and share concerns. Palliative Care aims at **diminishing** the impact of the crises around terminal illness and death, it **cannot resolve** them.

Objectives in music therapy are to be reflected upon in the same perspective. Music will be presented in its magnitude and various forms as a catalyst and stimulus to facilitate the intricate processes of a person's continual adjustment to lifethreatening illness and impending death. **Music therapy thus aims at diminishing the impact of the crises around terminal illness and death, not resolving them.** The essence lies in the focus on particular situations at a given moment. Ted Rosenthal, in "How Could I Not Be Among You," (25) pointedly captures the patient's dilemma in the everchanging circumstances when he describes how, while suffering from acute leukemia, he was never able to synchronize his feelings with the information that came to him about his physical condition and how every bit of information altered his feelings about himself in terms of survival and in relationship to the future or even the given moment.

Thus, the music therapist has to be wary of delving into patient and family issues which cannot be resolved. Continuity of the therapeutic process cannot be assured in this context, and we need to remind ourselves that patients rarely ask for therapy as such. Our mandate is to make every effort to diminish the impact of terminal disease and to accompany the patient in ways best suiting his lifestyle and way of thinking.

At the same time, however, the therapist will have to take risks in motivating or challenging the patient.* While risk-taking is an integral part of therapeutic intervention, it is again not simple in the context of dying. I can only presume the patient's very intimate feelings and perception, for I have never been terminally ill. My concept of the meaning of life, just as the patient's, differs from everyone's "...from day to day and from hour to hour..." (to use Victor Frankl's words). In this light, risk-taking has to be carefully considered in relationship to the patient's total care and not simply as a therapeutic technique.

In my personal experience I have found that patients welcomed my risked initiatives when they stemmed from careful observation and broad understanding of their predicament. In retrospect I realize that I occasionally risked pushing issues because of perceived role expectations and each time the patient reacted adversly. Miss Bernard's care gives such an example:

> I knew the patient from the consultation service, where listening to her favorite piece, the Beethoven String Septet (26), had led her to review much of her life, her dreams and her disappointments with me. Her accounts portrayed her as an energetic, independent lady who now, faced with inactivity and slowly progressing illness, did not see much reason for continued living.
>
> As her body succumbed to illness, the values and desires dearly held during her former life gave way. For her, pain, suffering and loss of independence eroded meaning and denied dignity. She resented having to give the context of her dying, the defense of her dignity and the statement of her values over to others. (27)
>
> It was therefore not surprising that upon being discharged home she simply wanted to be left alone. Private duty nurses found caring for her extremely difficult despite the support of the PCS home care nurse. The latter asked me to see Miss Bernard at home since she had related easily with me in the hospital. During my first visit I hoped to play for her but she wasn't feeling well and refused any kind of music.

* see p. 8

A fellow music therapist accompanied me on my next visit and the patient again evaded music involvement. When my colleague and I later discussed the events, she wondered if I should not have risked to simply play for her. I mentioned my reticence to consider Miss Bernard's behavior merely as manipulation and to override it with my intervention at this time.

When I subsequently reflected on our conversation I decided I had likely taken the easy way out and next time would play my instrument to force the issue, persuing my mandate as a therapist as my colleague had suggested.

A week later the patient's physical condition was much the same but she was grouchy and unpleasant with the nurse who tried to give her a bedbath. I went to an adjourning room and started to play my flute (an instrument she liked) in the hope of distracting her attention from the nurse's task. At the sound of the first few notes Miss Bernard began to scream at the top of her voice and told me to leave.

When the Home Care nurse visited next, the patient insisted that she take the tapes and tape recorder back to hospital (equipment she had previously at least occasionally used) and tell me not to come back.

This experience left me feeling uneasy for quite some time. I knew that I had intervened in order to meet some imagined expectation of my competence as a music therapist rather than choosing to respect and abide by the patient's wish to be left alone.

With time I learned to confront my reactions more honestly and to deal with them in a more realistic perspective. The whole realm of risks and limits in terminal care, however, warrants continual exploration and soul searching and cannot be ignored.

PERCEPTION OF DEATH — IDENTIFICATION

The purpose of this book is not to elaborate extensively on death and dying, nevertheless this volume would be lacking if some basic reflections on the subject were not addressed as they pertain to the music therapist.

Feifel and other authors consider death a key issue of life and advocate the conviction that in the last analysis all human behavior of consequence is a response to the problem of death. (28) (29) Becker takes this statement a bit further in maintaining that much of human activity is designed to avoid the fatality of death or to overcome it by denying in some way that it is the final destiny for humankind. (30)

In working with a dying patient we are unavoidably confronted with our own finiteness. The extent to which we face this reality will largely influence our coping and stress patterns. Inevitably we must look at some of the influences that have shaped our personal concept of and reactions to death as we witness the search for meaning and the struggle with pain and illness in others. Memories and associations will surface in us, yet we should not let them get in the way of our perception of the patient's plight, nor should we try to resolve our own unfinished business in palliative care work. At the same time we cannot help but be invaded by our own fears, anxieties and feelings even after extensive reflection, analysis and rationalization.

I am fortunate to have grown up in a small Swiss village where death was not hidden away and where customs and rituals helped to integrate dying into the context of living. For instance: when the mother of one of my classmates in grade six died suddenly, we students decided to offer a wreath as a token of our sympathy. I remember the afternoon spent in the forest with twenty other children searching for perfect pine bows, greenery and flowers. Without assistance we created a decorative ring, symbol of eternity and love, while occasionally reflecting on the unexpected death.

The group charged four of us to deliver the wreath to the house and we accepted the task rather hesitantly. The father of our friend opened the door, welcomed us and simply invited us to come upstairs and place our gift near his wife's body. She lay in a simple coffin, draped in a sheet surrounded by flowers and wreaths in the master bedroom, arranged for this occasion. I remember feeling awkward but deeply touched as we stood in silence with the bereaved family for a few minutes. They then ushered us to the door with much thanks for our gesture.

The following day our class joined the procession of mourners, relatives, neighbors and friends behind the horse-drawn hearse which slowly moved from the home towards the church. The ringing church bells announced the funeral event to everyone in the village where, in the ensuing weeks and months, the grief of this family would be respected.

In my work with dying patients I could draw and reflect on this experience which had helped me to see and understand the death event as an integral part of life; to allow myself to feel the sadness, grief and pain with the patient or a relative and yet stay detached enough to remain an effective helper. The music therapist in the palliative care/hospice setting has to allow him or herself to feel the patient's predicament and state of being in order to approximate appropriate music intervention. Rational judgement and choice alone will not permit us to explore all the dimensions of music which might reach the individual nor the depth of their concern, anguish or fear.

Daring to feel, however, makes us more vulnerable and leads to identification which, in dealing with dying, can be threatening. In the quiet of my living room or in philosophical discussions with friends I am convinced that death magnifies life and that I have faced its inevitability. When I stand at the bedside of a mother of two teenage children, whose face and body is disfigured by unsightly tumors, I cannot help the identification and find it hard to face that reality and to calm gnawing fears. I know that there is no way of hiding this fact. A sensitive patient will be aware of my feelings, a reality reflected in Ted Rosenthal's statement that he never really saw what fear was until he saw it in the eyes of those who looked at him.(31)

Identification is an unavoidable reality in caring for the dying. The therapist must acknowledge the undercurrents of occasional anxiety and fear in this regard and deal with them rather than suppress them. Now and then the sharing of such concerns symbolizes significant meaning as the plea of a dying student nurse to her colleagues suggests:

> "If only we could be honest, both admit of our fears, touch one another. If you really care, would you lose so much of your valuable professionalism if you even cried with me? Just person to person? Then, it might not be so hard to die - in a hospital - with friends close by." (32)

EMOTIONAL EQUILIBRIUM

The music therapist as a musician and artist, in contrast to other health professionals, can permit him or herself to be free and more at ease in the intuitive and emotional spheres of interaction, and to use these attributes within the professional mandate. The challenge, however, is to carefully distinguish emotional sensitivity from sentimentality on one hand, and on the other not to disregard emotional experience and insight which, while intangible, are yet significant for the sake of objective detachment.

Since the music therapist's media, music, is an emotionally charged instrument and circumstances in terminal care are equally emotionally intense, we have to handle music with particular humility and respect. We must use it with respect enough not to stereotype patients by our own prejudices and statistics, and with humility enough not to want to invade feelings of others because of our own needs.

The mushroom-like growth of the hospice movement in recent years has led to an intense, at times all but morbid, preoccupation with death and dying. The more experienced I have become, the more I am filled with concern about the many experts in various fields who seem to have all the answers to the best way of dying. I have met some of these "experts" in music therapy circles and fear that "death and dying music therapy" for them is seen as a sensational new subject to be theorized about in order to boost the music therapy profile or as an area of work through which they hope to solve their personal issues.

In my role as the first music therapist of the Royal Victoria Hospital's Palliative Care Service, I often felt the weight of the "fish bowl image" because this service is viewed around the world as an important model in terminal care. The more I learned from patients and staff about the intricacies of whole-person care for a dying individual however, the more mindful I became of **my responsibility as a music therapist not to misuse the potency of music nor the power of the therapeutic relationship established through music.** . I found it helpful to repeatedly ask the questions:

Whose needs am I fulfilling, the patient's or mine?

Whose "program" am I following, the patient's or mine?

Such questioning tended to balance my emotional and professional involvement.

While we must strive for a healthy emotional equilibrium with regard to the music therapy/therapist/patient relationships, we, at the same time, have to watch our own feeling barometer. We unconsciously assimilate a part of each situation and with unceasing exposure to suffering, pain, sadness and grief, such absorbed feelings may suddenly surface in unexpected ways unrelated to the work environment.

I remember stealing to my room for a good cry in the midst of a holiday at a music camp where I was thoroughly enjoying myself. Subsequently I questioned myself about this seemingly inappropriate emotional outburst. In reflecting on events that might have precipitated my tears, I suddenly realized that during the weeks prior to my holiday I had been involved in very complex sad cases with young patients and had witnessed several deaths. Even though I had acknowledged some sadness at the time, the work pace had impeded further attention to my feelings of sadness. Inevitably they surfaced in unrelated circumstances and obliged me to address the issue of unresolved grief. Fortunately I was aware of such experiences from accounts of some of my colleagues, which helped me place my reactions in an appropriate context. The holiday situation, at the same time, facilitated renewal and distancing. When the therapist experiences emotional overload during ongoing work, it is important to seek staff support or, if necessary, to request a short respite period.

PROFESSIONAL CONCERNS

Throughout this volume I have referred to the complexities of situations, diversity of patient population, divergence of needs and the intricacies of the music therapist's role. I cannot think of other clinical settings where the same magnitude of dimensions has to be considered, and I realize that these circumstances thoroughly strain the music therapist's professional skills and knowledge.

I had previously worked in settings where the patient group was fairly homogeneous and was each time able to supplement appropriately my existing music repertoire. During the first few months on the Palliative Care Service I desperately tried to find and learn new music which had significant meaning for various patients. Several times I spent hours in music libraries and music stores locating a particular piece, rushed home to practice in the hope of playing the music for a patient a couple of days later, and then found the person disinterested or too ill to benefit from the music! For every piece found and learned there was a new patient who related to completely different music again and for a while I was convinced that my skills were totally inadequate for this work! Only when I analyzed the problem carefully did I realize why I felt so overwhelmed. The age of the patients I worked with varied from eighteen to ninety years; their ethnic background, besides English and French Canadian, could be from just about every country around the world, representing enormous diversity in customs and beliefs around illness, life, faith and music. All social strata were represented, from the highly sophosticated intellectual to the street vagrant!

It simply is impossible to develop a repertoire that could encompass such diversity. Besides, I was neither Jean-Pierre Rampal nor James Galway, Arthur Rubenstein nor Alfred Cortot; and these artists had such significant meaning for some patients that they would have considered other interpretations unsatisfactory.

I quickly learned that patients did not necessarily enjoy live music, and that if I walked into a room with my flute in hand they invariably were forced to become extremely apologetic if they didn't want music. It took one patient weeks to tell me she really didn't like flute music, even though I had only played for her with her consent!

A further issue that made me question my professional competence was the fact that I seemed to spend much time talking to patients instead of music making with them. Improvisation, which I had hoped to use often, was only very infrequently an appropriate therapeutic technique with these very ill patients. I certainly needed to adjust my expectations in this regard.

Will I ever know how to respond adequately and appropriately in the many awkward moments? This question preoccupied me for a long time. Only gradually did I learn to **be** instead of to quickly want **to become,** and with this approach I found answers. Yet I now understand that it will never be completely easy to answer the person who looks you straight in the eyes and asks: "Am I dying now?"

Despite ready support from my colleagues in the various disciplines, I couldn't help occasionally feeling the professional isolation and loneliness as the sole music therapist in the hospital. Contact with my fellow music therapists who worked in different settings only partially filled this void. Nurses discussed their approaches and problems with other nurses, physicians consulted other physicians over medical issues. As the music therapist, however, I had to rely on my own resources and risk new advances which, while challenging, were also draining, wearing and at times rather lonely.

Gilbert, in the Journal of NAMT wrote:

> "To establish music therapy as a viable service in death and dying, practicing music therapists must confirm the benefits of music therapy in terminal illness by demonstrating its effectiveness. Music therapists should concentrate upon devising effective techniques for using music in the death and dying process." (33)

Had I sought effectiveness and techniques only, I doubt if music would have had the depth of meaning experienced by some patients. I consider "the dying process" still very much a mystery with many unpredictabilities in the medical and human spheres. Kubler-Ross suggest that to be a therapist to a dying patient makes us aware of the uniqueness of each individual in the vast sea of humanity. (34) Music reflects the depth of experience of humanity and is accessible to the uniqueness in each person. The challenge for the music therapist in terminal care lies in searching for ways to link the uniqueness of music with the uniqueness of the dying patient.

As music therapists we are guides on our patient's journey; guarding, supporting and aiding them in identifying meaningful themes. (35) In the palliative/hospice care setting our own journey towards growth and understanding of the meaning of life is an integral part of music therapy. It has to be a thread that weaves itself through our interactions with patients yet which should not become entangled around our own needs.

Music is a symbol and a source
It comforts and soothes
It inspires and delights
It feeds

It weeps
And builds solid structures
From tears

It lights
To vision
Beyond our understanding

It dares to dream
To reflect and clarify

Music reminds us of our common heartbeat
Through time and space

It celebrates our eccentricities,
Our uniqueness

It leads the way to the future
Without denying the past

It laughs with new laughter
Never laughed before
Yet resembling an echo
From some distant hall

It floats and suspends
To calm, coax and cleanse

It provides a framework
From which to make choices

It is the history of sound
Of the continuity of life

It breathes
It stretches, yawns
To a new day

Music transforms
If we will only hear

C. BEREZNAK KENNY

THE SCOPE OF MUSIC

THE SCOPE OF MUSIC

Years ago I thought I lived, felt and understood some of the essence of music. Later, as a student in the improvisation course in my music therapy training at the Guildhall School of Music and Drama in London, I realized that I had not even begun to understand musical experience and subsequently explored it more deeply. In my early work as a music therapist I yet discovered new dimensions of music's potency; but only in the complexity of palliative care, faced with the dichotomies of each situation and each patient, did I begin to grasp the real magnitude of music.

In this context it is not enough to think of music in terms of frequency, intensity, tone color, intervals, harmony, rhythm and tempo only. Neither is it enough to consider solely its physiological impact on us. To merely keep music as expression in view or to underline mainly its intrusive and reaching qualities would limit its design. Only if we contemplate music as an integral thread running through life will we see all of its potential as a therapeutic agent in terminal care. The dying process affects the whole person; body, mind, heart and soul. Music's intricate association to all of human experience throughout the ages enables it to touch the "total person" (body, mind, heart and soul) like a mythic artery:

> "The MYTHIC ARTERY is an image, a way of thinking about music, which will aid us in our search for health. The Mythic Artery is liquid. It is vibrating. It is full of life-giving nutrients and chemicals. It quenches our thirst. It goes to and comes from the heart. It travels through all of time and contains the wisdom of the ages. It restores. It re-creates and cleanses. It brings us to the community of man and life as a whole. It gives us power, strength, humility. It is a stream which winds back through all the ages to the essence of our beginnings — our first heart beat, the first story of our existence. It allows us to be part of the whole and yet unique within the travelling undulations of time. It recycles. It purifies. It transforms. This is the music of life." (36)

The music therapist in hospice care cannot simply turn to music therapy textbooks to find applicable techniques for using music, he or she has to search for the thread of music in the life of each person and in this process discover where it wove itself into meaning for that individual.

Music has meaning in one's life for many reasons. Let us mention but a few:

- it has roots in history and discovery
- it was and is, created and played by man, thus providing links to human experience
- it is represented in the arts (religious, ancient, contemporary arts)
- it reflects periods in time
- it speaks of philosophies of life of different spheres of the world
- it mirrors people and their worlds, their way of expression, with which we can identify and to which we can relate
- we relate to a composer, a conductor, an interpreter, an instrument or music itself
- music is a voice
a word
a gesture
a story
a dream

- for some it is a place
  an era
  an event
- music is symbolic language tied into emotions

Human beings can tune in and connect with music at any level appropriate to their personality, intellect, need or wish at any given moment regardless of age, race or creed. They tune in and connect with music either superficially, emotionally, cerebrally, intellectually or at innermost depth.

The music therapist has to be a facilitator who provides opportunities where music, in any of these dimensions, can be accessible to a patient at whatever level and in whatever mode most significant to the individual in a given situation. Much of the power of music lies in its intimate connection to the uniqueness of one's being and the therapist has to learn to trust music to do the job of healing, comforting or nurturing growth. Music "theraps" frequently fare better than the most skilled therapist. The latter simply has to set the appropriate stage for this process to take place.

I have met few patients who wanted to talk directly about dying for any length of time. I have met even fewer who wanted to sing, hear sung or write about death or talk about death and rebirth symbolized in music. Yet, many patients did convey their anxieties around death and dying using symbolic language in stories about their lives, their music, their plans, their hopes and their dreams. Such language was more comfortable and less threatening, and caregivers could still hear the concerns and respond to them. In this communication through symbols however, music will reach far beyond human interaction. It can allow us to travel to the edge of life and back again, to experience transition, a moment of change and the mystery of transformation. Music nourishes like oxygen. It speaks of the continuity of things. It is a thread from the past, through the present, to the future. The reader might want to review the preceeding case studies with these reflections in mind.

We must see music in a holistic perspective and go beyond traditional definitions if it is to serve as a therapeutic medium in the intricacies of terminal care. It is this magnitude that favors its mulitfaceted scope.

Music is

- universal
- feeling
- silence
- resonance
- emotion
- comfort
- escape
- sound
- imagination
- catalyst
- expression
- security
- conflict
- association

- Music is an intruder, aggressor, facilitator
- Music communicates what can and cannot be spoken
- Music is a vital force, difficult to resist
- Music is an art; creative, expressive, dynamic, spontaneous, flexible
- Music stimulates, moves, relaxes, both physically and psychologically
- Music is present, past ,future
- Music is a way to go beyond the confines of everyday living
- Music demands inner silence and hearing
- Music is personal, yet universal

The music therapist who perceives music in this holistic way has to have felt and feel, has to have experienced and experience, has to have explored and explore music very personally. He or she needs to be a musical being who is able to tune into the musical being of the patient. In palliative care, however, tuning into the musical being alone does not suffice. We concomitantly have to tune carefully into the experience of dying as it is lived by each individual. At all times we will have to respect the person's own way.

"Everything can be taken from a man but one thing; the last of human freedoms — to choose one's attitude in any given set of circumstances, to choose one's own way." (37)

VICTOR E. FRANKL

music
SOUND
SILENCE
CATALYST
ESCAPE
FEELING
RESONANCE
ASSOCIATION
IMAGINATION
SECURITY
COMFORT
UNIVERSAL
SENSUAL
EXPRESSION
EMOTION
CONFLICT
SPIRITUAL

APPENDIX I

FOOTNOTES

(For complete references, please see the following pages.)

1) AJEMIAN (p. 91) *
2) Ibid (p. 281)
3) Ibid (p. 293)
4) Ibid (p. 323)
5) Ibid (p. 362)
6) Ibid (p. 367)
7) HAMPSON (p. 402, 403)
8) RAPHAEL
9) COUSINS
10) SIMINTON
11) BONNY
12) THOSHIBA
13) MOZART
14) SCHUBERT
15) GALWAY
16) MORISOD
17) ENVIRONMENT
18) AJEMIAN (p. 276)
19) Ibid (p. 457-507)
20) MARANTZ
21) BOW HARP
22) CHOROI HARP
23) WEISMAN (p. 116)
24) ARIES (p. 13)
25) ROSENTHAL (p. 73)
26) BEETHOVEN
27) CASSEL (p. 45)
28) FEIFEL (preface)
29) GORDON (p. 3)
30) BECKER (p. ix)
31) ROSENTHAL (p. 28)
32) ANONYMOUS (p. 336)
33) GILBERT
34) KUBLER ROSS (p. 276)
35) KENNY, C. (p. 123)
36) Ibid (p. 55)
37) FRANKL (p. 104)

* page numbers refer to pages in the respective resource books

BIBLIOGRAPHY

AJEMIAN, I., *THE RVH MANUAL ON PALLIATIVE/HOSPICE CARE.* (Ajemian, I. and Mount, B. ed.) New York, Arno Press 1980.

ALVIN, J., *MUSIC THERAPY.* London, Hutchinson & Co. 1975.

AMIES, D. & MOUNT, B., LETTERS TO THE EDITOR, in CANADIAN MEDICAL ASSOCIATION JOURNAL, vol. 120, 1979.

ANONYMOUS, *AMERICAN JOURNAL OF NURSING.* The American Journal of Nursing Company, February 1970.

ARIES, P., DEATH INSIDE OUT, in *DEATH INSIDE OUT.* The Hastings Center Report, (Steinfels P. and Veatch M. ed.) New York, Harper and Row, 1974.

BECKER, E., *THE DENIAL OF DEATH.* New York, McGraw-Hill Book Company, 1977.

BONNY, H. & SAVARY, R., *MUSIC AND YOUR MIND.* New York, Harper and Row, 1973.

CASSEL, E., DYING IN A TECHNOLOGICAL SOCIETY in *DEATH INSIDE OUT.* The Hastings Center Report. (Steinfels P. and Veatch M. ed.) New York, Harper and Row, 1974.

COUSINS, N., *AN ANATOMY OF AN ILLNESS* as preceived by the patient; reflections on healing and regeneration, New York, Norton, 1979.

FEIFEL, H., *NEW MEANINGS OF DEATH.* New York, McGraw-Hill Inc., 1977.

FRANKL, V., *MAN'S SEARCH FOR MEANING.* Boston, Beacon Press, 1963.

GILBERT, MUSIC THERAPY PERSPECTIVES ON DEATH AND DYING. *JOURNAL OF MUSIC THERAPY,* XIV(4), Lawrence, Kansas, National Association of Music Therapy Inc., 1977.

GORDON, R., SOCIAL ATTITUDES TO DEATH in *DYING AND CREATING* (Fordam M., Gordon R., Hubback J., Lambert K., ed.) London, The Society of Analytical Psychology, 1978.

HALPERN, S., *TUNING THE HUMAN INSTRUMENT.* Palo Alto, California, Spectrum Research Institute, 1978.

HAMEL, P., *THROUGH MUSIC TO THE SELF.* Wiltshire, Compton Press, 1976.

HAMPSON, A., PALLIATIVE CARE SERVICE BEREAVEMENT PROGRAM in *THE RVH MANUAL ON PALLIATIVE/HOSPICE CARE* (Ajemian, I. and Mount, B. ed.) New York, Arno Press, 1980.

KELEMAN, S., *LIVING YOUR DYING.* New York, Random House Press, 1974.

KENNY, C., *THE MYTHIC ARTERY,* The Magic of Music Therapy. Atascadera, California, Ridgeview Publishing Company, 1982.

KUBLER ROSS, E., *ON DEATH AND DYING.* New York, Macmillan, 1969.

KUBLER ROSS, E., *DEATH THE FINAL STAGE OF GROWTH.* New Jersey, Prentice Hall Inc., 1975.

MCNIFF, S., *THE ARTS AND PSYCHOTHERAPY.* Springfield, Illinois, Charles C. Thomas, 1981.

MUNRO S., & MOUNT, B., MUSIC THERAPY IN PALLIATIVE CARE in *THE CANADIAN MEDICAL ASSOCIATION JOURNAL,* vol. 119, 1978.

PRIESTLEY, M., *MUSIC THERAPY IN ACTION.* New York, St. Martin's Press, 1975.

RAPHAEL, B., PREVENTIVE INTERVENTION WITH RECENTLY BEREAVED, *ARCHIVES OF GENERAL PSYCHIATRY,* 1977, 1450-1454.

SIMONTON, C. et al, *GETTING WELL AGAIN:* A Step-by-Step Self Help Guide to Overcoming Cancer for Patients and Their Families. New York, Bantam, 1980.

VERDEAU-PAILLES, J., *LE BILAN PSYCHO-MUSICAL ET LA PERSONNALITE.* Courlay France, Editions J.M. Fuzeau, 1981.

WEISMAN, A., THE PSYCHIATRIST AND THE INEXORABLE in *NEW MEANINGS OF DEATH.* Feifel, H., New York, McGraw-Hill Inc., 1977.

REFERENCES

MUSIC:

BACH, J.S.	AIR ON THE G-STRING, CBS - XM 7501, ARIOSO FROM CANTATA N. 156, COLUMBIA MG 31261
BEETHOVEN, L.V.	SEPTET IN Eb, Op. 20, NONESUCH N-78015
GALWAY, J.	SONGS OF THE SEASHORE, RCA RECORDS, ARK-1 3534, 1980
MORISOD, A.	PERCÉ, Et les oiseaux chantaient, KOSMOS: KOSX-191, Side 2
MOZART, W.A.	ANDANTE, PIANO CONCERTO N. 21, Deutsche Grammophone 138783
SCHUBERT, F.	ANDANTE CON MOTO, STRING QUARTET in d minor, ("Death and the Maiden"), CBS 3701

ENVIRONMENT SERIES: ATLANTIC/WEA SC 66001
SYNTONIC RESEARCH, INC.

INSTRUMENTS

BOW HARP,	KELISCHEK WORKSHOP FOR HISTORICAL INSTRUMENTS, BRASSTOWN, N.C. 28902, U.S.A.
CHOROI HARP,	KUNST UND SPIEL, VERSANDABTEILUNG, HOHENZOLLERN-STRASSE 14, 8000 MUNICH, W. GERMANY

EQUIPMENT

MARANTZ,	SUPERSCOPE C-170
THOSHIBA,	KT-S2

RELAXATION TAPES

These tapes were prepared for use in the following situation:

- anxiety attacks
- extreme shortness of breath
- insomnia
- restlessness
- difficult nursing procedures

Music selection was based on rhythm (slow, steady pulse), long phrases, little dynamic variation and emotional components. One selection was repeated over the entire length of one tape (30 minutes) in order to minimize variation of pulse.

EXAMPLES:

Mozart, W.A.	ANDANTE from PIANO CONCERTO N. 21
Bach, J.S.	AIR ON THE G-STRING
Bach, J.S.	ARIOSO from CANTATA N. 156
Morisod, A.	"ET LES OISEAUX CHANTAIENT"

APPENDIX II

The following article and letters are reprinted with permission from the Canadian Medical Association Journal and are included in this manual to document possible reactions to the subject of music therapy in palliative care.

Music therapy in palliative care

S. MUNRO,* LGSM (MT); B. MOUNT,† MD, FRCS[C]

Initial observations regarding the use of music therapy at one hospital in the palliative care of patients with advanced malignant disease are presented. In the hands of a trained music therapist, music has proven to be a potent tool for improving the quality of life. The diversity of its potential is particularly suited to the diversity of the challenges — physical, psychosocial and spiritual — that these patients present.

On présente des premières observations sur l'usage dans un hôspital de la musique comme traitment palliatif des patients souffrant de maladie maligne avancée. Aux mains d'un musicothérapeute entrainé, la musique s'est avérée un instrument puissant pour l'amélioration de la qualité de la vie. La diversité de son potentiel convient particulièrement à la diversité des défis physique, psychosocial et spirituel que présentent ces patients.

There would be no music and no need for it if it were possible to communicate verbally that which is easily communicated musically.

— E. Thayer Gaston, 1958

The program in music therapy of the Royal Victoria Hospital's palliative care service ‡ was begun in September 1977. The aim of this pilot project was to define further the potential of music therapy in meeting the needs of the terminally ill and their families, with a trained music therapist working as a member of a multidisciplinary health care team.

The purpose of this paper is to outline the rationale of using music therapy in palliative care and to offer preliminary observations on the impact of this underused therapeutic tool.

Music therapy

Definition

Music therapy is the controlled use of music, its elements and their influences on the human being to aid in the physiologic, psychologic and emotional integration of the individual during the treatment of an illness or disability.

History

Music and medicine have been closely associated for centuries.[2] For primitive societies music played a significant role in the priest-practitioner's powers. The Greeks' use of music and medicaments in conjunction with oracular utterances was an early foray into the field of psychosomatic medicine. Pythagoras believed that if one used music in daily life in a prescribed manner, it would make a salutary contribution to one's health. This led him to investigate the physics of sound and to develop the fundamentals of today's tonal system. "Psychocatharsis" — purging or purifying the emotions through music — was recognized and used by Aristotle. With the Renaissance came the study of anatomy and an emphasis on observing the cause-and-effect nature of phenomena. First accounts of the influence of music on breathing, blood pressure, muscular activity and digestion came from this period.

While the traditional close association between music and medical practice was largely forgotten in the technologic explosion of the 20th century, the last 2 decades have seen a resurgence in interest and research to evaluate the physiologic and psychologic effects of music.[3,4]

From the palliative care service, Royal Victoria Hospital, Montreal

* *Music therapist*

† *Director, palliative care service; associate professor of surgery, McGill University, Montreal*

Reprint requests to: Dr. B. Mount, Palliative care service, Royal Victoria Hospital, 687 Pine Ave. W, Montreal, PQ H3A 1A1

‡ *The palliative care service was instituted at the Royal Victoria Hospital, an 850-bed teaching hospital affiliated with McGill University, in January 1975 in an attempt to better meet the needs (physical, psychologic, social and spiritual) of terminally ill patients and their families. The four clinical branches of the service are an inpatient ward (the palliative care unit), a home care program, a bereavement follow-up service and a consultation service. The palliative care service is staffed by a multidisciplinary team that includes physicians, nurses, volunteers, a social worker, a chaplain, a physiotherapist, a psychiatrist, a psychologist and a music therapist, as well as research and administrative staff.*[1]

The music therapist

While it has been recognized since the days of David and Saul that any motivated person, irrespective of training, may effectively use music in ministering to the sick, the term "music therapist" refers to a specially trained individual whose intervention is based on a thorough knowledge of all facets of music (historical, theoretic and practical), the behavioral sciences, treatment and educational models, and accepted therapeutic approaches.

Today therapists use music to facilitate specific behavioral changes. Music therapy is applied in a variety of clinical settings where music therapists are part of the treatment team: the fields include psychiatry (in psychoanalysis and the treatment of drug addiction, alcoholism and personality disorders), special education (in patients with retardation, learning disabilities, emotional disturbance or physical handicaps), rehabilitation, gerontology, speech disorders, kinetics and anesthesiology.[5-13]

Methods

The music therapist in the palliative care service has used a variety of musical instruments (flute, organ, violin, bow harp, tambourine) both in performing for and with the patients, and in having others perform for them. A component mobile stereophonic system for playing records and tapes can be used with groups or individuals. Earphones are available for use with this system or with small tape recorders for the bedside.

A library of taped music is available to provide a wide range of music matching tastes, moods and ethnic backgrounds. Large typed songsheets and hymnals are used at informal get-togethers as well as planned religious services.

A large portion of the therapist's time is spent in listening to the patients and in nurturing the discussions arising from the musical interaction. Other means of self-expression, such as making collages, drawing to music, and family and group activities and discussions, further the expression of feelings.

The therapist is an active participant in ward meetings, where therapeutic interventions are planned. She sees patients in the palliative care unit and those receiving home care or consultation services at the request of other team members. At present, criteria for involving the music therapist include extreme anxiety, alarming withdrawal, language barriers, difficulties of interaction and intractable pain.

Meeting the needs of the terminally ill

Saunders[14] has emphasized the need to address psychosocial and spiritual issues in addition to medical needs if excellence in symptom control is to be achieved for the terminally ill. The experience of the palliative care service has corroborated this observation.[15]

The work of Kubler-Ross[16] suggests that in intergrating the knowledge of their finiteness, patients and families, and to some extent care-givers, go through a series of emotional stages or mental adjustments. Friedman[17] proposed that these adjustments must be made in each area of man's existence — physical, psychologic, social and spiritual.

The multidimensional qualities of music allow it to touch many levels of consciousness. It can act as a catalyst in mobilizing deep feelings and can assist in both verbal and nonverbal communication.[18, 19]

Considering the accepted potential of music therapy and the recognized needs of those requiring palliative care, one can predict a broad variety of uses of music therapy in these patients:

- Physical
  - — promoting muscular relaxation
  - — breaking the vicious circle of chronic pain by relieving anxiety and depression and thus altering the perception of pain
  - — facilitating physical participation in activities to the degree possible
- Psychologic
  - — reinforcing identity and self-concept
  - — altering the patient's mood, including easing anxiety and lessening depression
  - — helping the patient recall past significant events
  - — providing a nonverbal means of expressing a broad range of recognized and unconscious feelings
  - — reinforcing reality
  - — expressing fantasy
  - — as a direct appeal to the emotions
- Social
  - — as a means of socially acceptable self-expression
  - — as a bridge across cultural differences and isolation
  - — as a bond and sense of community with family members and others, past and present, through the mental associations aroused
  - — as a link to the patient's life before the illness
  - — providing an opportunity to participate in a group
  - — as entertainment and diversion
- Spiritual
  - — providing means of expressing spiritual feelings and feeling comforted and reassured
  - — providing an avenue for expressing doubts, anger, fear of punishment, and questions on the ultimate meaning of life.

Case reports

Case 1

A 32-year-old unmarried woman, who had been dynamic and outgoing when well, was admitted to the palliative care unit 6 months after undergoing hysterectomy for carcinoma of the cervix with widespread lymphatic involvement. Postoperative radiation therapy and chemotherapy had had no apparent impact on the rapid progression of the disease.

Problems at the time of admission included severe anasarca, pain incompletely controlled by narcotics taken by mouth, insomnia, constipation, dysphagia, urinary incontinence, dyspnea and, of particular distress to patient, family and staff, intermittent severe anxiety attacks characterized by extreme physical tension and overwhelming panic. During the attacks she would lie rigid for extended periods with clenched fists held a little off the bed, and would show signs of anguish and overall physical discomfort; she could not relax or sleep.

She was aware of and wished to talk about her diagnosis and prognosis, volunteering that she wished she would die quickly. She had an attentive family. Careful positioning of the bed, with elevation of the arms, meticulous mouth and skin care, including regular turning and the massaging of her back and legs, adjustments in the dose of narcotic analgesics, the use of laxatives, urinary tract catheterization, chest physiotherapy and a liquid diet provided symptomatic relief. Verbal reassurance and the physical presence of family and staff did not, however, ease the severity of her anxiety attacks.

Following an assessment interview the music therapist prepared an audio-tape with a variety of musical selections aimed at inducing relaxation. Selection criteria for the music included a steady reassuring rhythm, low-frequency tones, soothing orchestral effects and a comforting, serene melody.

The patient's degree and rapidity of response on first hearing the tape were impressive. Within a few minutes her facial expression relaxed and her respirations deepened and became regular; her hands relaxed and lowered to rest on the bed, and she fell into a deep sleep. The entrance of staff members into the room failed to disturb her, yet as soon as the tape ended she awakened. Her hands moved off the bed once again and signs of distress returned. In the ensuing conversation she acknowledged that she was afraid of sleeping, stating that she was not ready to "let go". This comment opened the way for a discussion of her fears with the therapist. The tape was repeatedly played at her request over the following days. Relaxation and easing of distress was noted on each occasion.

One day, when the patient was comatose and unresponsive, the therapist, for the first time, sat at her bedside and played several soothing selections on the flute. The patient did not react visibly to the music. However, the following day, after she regained consciousness, she asked the therapist to play the flute for her. When questioned she said she did not remember hearing the music the day before.

Comment: This patient demonstrated clearly the multifactorial character of chronic pain that led Saunders to coin the term "total pain". Physical and psychologic components played major roles in her distress, though social and spiritual issues also required resolution. The music impressively completed the previously inadequate pharmacologic and interpersonal interventions. Her awareness of and subsequent unconscious recall of music played to her when she was clinically unresponsive is an important reminder that unconscious patients should be related to and addressed as if fully alert.

Case 2

A woman was transferred to the palliative care unit expecting to be subsequently discharged to home care. Two years earlier she had undergone right mastectomy for breast carcinoma, followed by cyclic chemotherapy. For the 2 months prior to admission she had experienced increasing anorexia and weakness. Mulitple skeletal and hepatic metastases were present. Symptom control was easily achieved.

For the 3½ months before she died her continually deteriorating physical status coupled with the absence of adequate support at home prevented discharge. In spite of this disappointment she was always socially pleasant. The nurses described her as "reserved; very English; quiet; knows own mind; doesn't express her feelings very openly". Her relation with the staff, other patients and their families, and even her own family were seen as somewhat distant, although always socially correct.

Recognizing that the patient avoided verbal communication of her feelings yet needed to relate more meaningfully, the therapist took the patient to the quiet lounge frequently used for music therapy, gave her a variety of magazines, and encouraged her to "let the music sink in" while selecting photographs from the magazines that seemed meaningful to her. The music was Schubert's string quartet *Der Tod und Das Mädchen.*

In her own words, the resulting collage reflected "the continuation of life: Europe, the old country, where there is culture, art and architecture. Then people left. They came here and settled, building small houses and 'cardboard' churches that in the end are only empty shells. Well, life goes on and man still thinks he is in control." Pointing to a picture of an abandoned house she said: "This is the most significant picture for me". She did not want to expand on the reasons for this statement. In the following weeks an unhappy family situation was revealed; it included divorce proceedings for both daughters, tensions in her relations with her immature son, who was unemployed, and estrangement from her invalid husband. The patient had expressed nonverbally what she could never admit to verbally.

The powers of association that music may unlock were demonstrated when the patient reflected on her youth and the English countryside while listening to Beethoven's *Pastoral.* When the symphony ended she hummed a brief melodic phrase from something she had sung in a choir as a schoolgirl. She went over it repeatedly but could not recall the title of words. From the remembered phrases the therapist identified the Pilgrims' Chorus from *Taunhaüser* by Wagner. She obtained a recording sung in German and played it for the patient, who was deeply pleased but still could not remember the words. After several hearings she suddenly recalled the lyrics of one line of the entire chorus; the line she had initially hummed: "but pain and death I do not fear". The patient and therapist then reflected together on the many implications of her illness and on her impending death. It was that same chorus that provided great support for the patient later, just before she died.

Comment: The ability of music to assist in verbal and nonverbal communication and to bring to the fore significant past associations renders it a powerful tool in assisting patients in their attempt to come to terms with reality.

Case 3

An 84-year-old woman was admitted to the palliative care unit 3 months after clinical diagnosis of abdominal carcinoma, presumed to be of pancreatic origin. The woman firmly refused all investigations and treatment and was referred to the unit with diarrhea, fecal and urinary incontinence, weakness, anorexia, a coccygeal decubitus ulcer, apparent confusion and distress.

The use of pancreatic enzymes, antidiarrheal agents, physiotherapy for progressive mobilization and assistance in transfer, urinary tract catheterization, skin care and repeated gentle orientation reminders led to a lessening of symptomatic distress. Three overriding considerations remained, however: (a) a stubborn resistance to eating hospital food; (b) an antisocial and withdrawn emotional makeup (she was described by the admitting physician as "very negative and resistant to all contacts"); and (c) a marked language barrier. The patient spoke Russian and apparently only a few words of French.

The refusal to eat was overcome following consultation with the family, who supplied a continual diet of baked or boiled potatoes (mashed were refused) and black bread.

Following an initial interview with the patient, the music therapist recorded: "She seems to be extremely difficult to handle; language barrier; hostility; paranoia; apparent confusion making positive interaction with her almost impossible."

The therapist then obtained a recording of music sung by a Russian choir. While playing it she handed the patient the record cover, with its printed Russian and English text. As the first strains of the initial chorus swelled to fill the room the patient's facial expression changed to an alert, proud look and she seemed to grow in stature. With dignity and secure intonation she read the Russian text aloud, her diction perfect. A pause followed, then the patient, in adequate French, told the story of her childhood as a member of an aristocratic Russian family, where music, dance, literature and art were of great importance. She went on to speak of her bitterness at the loss of prestige, homeland, beauty and, eventually, health. In the ensuing days music was frequently the bridge to otherwise impossible communication.

Comment: Music opened channels of communication that enabled the staff to encounter the positive aspects of the patient's personality within the negative shell presented on initial interaction. We have observed that patients often return to the music and language of their childhood in the last stage of their illness, even when they have not spoken that language for years. Many feel extremely embarrassed about this "regression" and need reassurance about the feared "loss of face". Songs of childhood within many cultures reflect secure relationships (lullabies and love songs), spontaneous activity and learning (action songs), dreams and fantasies of children, and reflections on deeply rooted folk traditions. Their use permits a return to childhood without loss of face. For the dying it is often extremely difficult to express feelings about the impending separation from loved ones. Songs stating these themes in their first-learned language give patients an important stimulus to help them express such sentiments.

Case 4

A 70-year-old man was transferred to the palliative care unit 1 month after radiologic diagnosis of lung carcinoma with multiple bony metastases and associated pneumonitis. He had a resolving cutaneous pemphigoid eruption and weakness of his legs on admission.

While both patient and family were aware of his diagnosis and prognosis, the patient tended not to discuss either. When seen by the music therapist he quipped, "Let's hear Nat King Cole; something jazzy — none of this quiet stuff!"

The "nursing care plan" notes observed: "Doesn't discuss illness prognosis with family." Over the following days, however, the presence of a supportive therapeutic milieu appeared to facilitate discussions with staff members once he got to know them. Nursing staff found that discussions that were initially superficial and flippant frequently evolved to a point that allowed more accurate expression of feelings.

During the week following admission, the patient witnessed the death of a patient in the same room. When he next met the music therapist he asked to be taken "to a quiet place to listen to music". From a selection of records he chose *Cello Pieces,* played by Pablo Casals, and Beethoven's *Pathetique.* At their completion he talked lightly about superficial matters, then, in progression, discussed illness in general, his own illness and impending death, and finally, his feelings about the death of his fellow patient.

Comment: Music chosen by a patient may reflect mood or be a defence mechanism. A shift in musical taste may reflect an alteration in mood; conversely, the therapist can induce such a shift in the selections used, to effect a gradual change in the patient's mood.

Case 5

A 53-year-old man was transferred to the palliative care unit 9 months after diagnosis of an anaplastic carcinoma of the sphenoid sinus. The patient had undergone transphenoidal resection and, following demonstration of local extension through the sella turcica, radiation therapy. Cyclic chemotherapy was subsequently instituted. Paraplegia and weakness in his arms due to metastases involving cervical vertebrae had developed 3 months before transfer.

The patient, of central European origin, was a very private individual who described himself as a perfectionist. Rarely one to express feelings, he had always found it easiest to relate to others through his work (accounting) and through the highly demanding standards he set for himself. He and his wife had two teenaged children.

At the time of admission to the unit the patient was emaciated, had a sacrococcygeal decubitus ulcer and was anorexic, as well as intermittently somewhat disoriented. He also had diplopia and pain in the neck and right shoulder. While he did raise questions relating to prognosis, he frequently showed florid denial regarding the severity of his disease. He was clearly depressed and anxious, was highly demanding of family and staff, and demonstrated a great need to retain control of his environment.

Symptom control was sought through various medications, including narcotics, dexamethasone, prochlorperazine, diazepam and laxatives. Nursing care included repeated gentle orientation cueing, frequent turning, mouth care and attention to the decubitus ulcer. An attempt was made to include the patient in decisions regarding daily routines, and nursing care was scheduled according to his wishes.

Counseling was provided for the patient's wife and children in view of the wife's anxiety and difficulty in making decisions and the children's feelings of guilt. The wife exhibited a great need to deny the severity of her husband's illness. Carefully planned supportive interactions with staff included, over many weeks, meetings and discussions with nurses, physicians, phychiatrist, chaplain, social worker and volunteers.

The music therapist played an important role in meeting the highly complex needs of this patient and his family. The patient's mask of intellectualization and control quickly fell when he requested and sang, in a strong baritone, some of his favourite songs. Tears flowed easily as he listened to: "I hear the gentle voices calling, old black Joe" (Stephen Foster). His choice and interpretation of songs revealed a very sensitive person struggling for understanding and acceptance of his condition. He clearly welcomed the opportunity to choose the music and express his feelings in this manner. Music had formed an important part of his life when well, and its availability during the last few weeks of his life proved to be very meaningful to him. When he sustained a pathologic fracture of the right humerus, his love for music was used to distract him from the discomfort during painful repositioning. The resultant decrease in muscle spasm and enhanced cooperation led him to a substantial decrease in the time spent on the physical care of this patient and supported staff-patient relations.

The use of liturgical music helped the whole family express the strong religious faith that supported them.

A further contribution of the music therapist became possible just before the patient's death, when, after gentle encouragement and assistance by the therapist, the patient planned and prepared a tape of his favourite songs for "my wife on our last anniversary".

Comment: This patient was able to express emotions that otherwise remained repressed, both through singing and through selecting recorded music. Music relieved physical pain and was a source of spiritual comfort. It also was a vehicle for the expression of important feelings between family members.

Case 6

A 19-year-old man had undergone resection of a poorly differentiated diffuse lymphocytic lymphoma causing stage II disease a year before the palliative care service was consulted. Palliative abdominal irradiation and chemotherapy were used with varying effect as the months passed. At the time of his last admission to hospital he had severe back pain and intermittent colicky abdominal pain. Chemotherapy produced no measurable response. His symptoms worsened, with intractable nausea, vomiting and pain, and extreme emotional stress for patient, family and medical staff. A progress note by the intern observed: "Pain in back, crampy pain in bowels, patient expresses anguish over his possible death, expresses wish to die rather than suffer more pain ... Assessment: Tumor unresponsive to chemotherapy, anxiety in extremis."

At this point the patient was seen in consultation by the palliative care service. A program of relaxation and music therapy had extremely good results in relieving his pain and anxiety. During the last week of his life he continued to have intractable vomiting of large amounts of gastric secretions owing to complete gastric outlet obstruction. He was unable to take allopurinol orally, and hyperuricemia when subsequent renal failure developed.

The intervention used with such striking benefits in this very receptive patient consisted of two elements: (a) the use of a simple form of guided imagery, * which was easily taught to family and medical staff; and (b) the playing of taped music selected by the therapist. The selections included were by Bach *(Air on the G-String,* excerpts from *The Little Suite,* a cello version of *Komm Susser Tod* and *Jesu, Joy of Man's Desiring),* Schubert *(Ave Maria).* Saint Saens *(Swan)* and Mozart (the *laudate dominum* from *The Vespers).*

During previous admissions the patient had insisted on listening only to an FM radio station playing "rock" music. As his pain and agitation increased he became intolerant to "his" music. The music therapist's notes following the first use of the tape read: "The patient was frantic to get more medication but was also tense and afraid that he couldn't relax at all anymore. The music and relaxation techniques helped to calm him in approximately 10 minutes *without extra medication.*

In the last days of his life the patient repeatedly requested that the tape be palyed. Analgesics were discontinued and the patient was managed with relaxation techniques and music therapy only. He was quite comfortable, not anxious, and able to talk with his family and many visitors. The nursing notes in his chart reflect the impressive effect this had on the patient, his family and the staff.

Comment: The profound impact of selected music by Bach, Schubert and other composers on a youth previously unreceptive to classical music suggests that music may be highly effective in relieving the anguish of "total pain" even when the listener has not previously been conditioned to that music. The use of simple guided imagery as an adjunct to music therapy was highly effective in this case.

Discussions and conclusions

Music therapy has made a significant contribution to a wide variety of palliative care problems. The presence of music in the hospital has been well received by patients and their families. It is often able to comfort when words are inadequate or inappropriate. It may provide a means of positive interaction and expression of feelings.

Music has, however, a very personal and intimate meaning for each individual, a fact that demands a great deal of respect. It is important to stress the need for careful assessment in the introduction and application of music with each patient. Man has little defence against the influence of music. Its impact often has far-reaching emotional and psychologic effects that need to be observed and channelled appropriately.

---

* *The patient is verbally encouraged to think of a particular image that matches the music — for example, ocean, surf, wind in the woods or a positive past experience.*

The occasion, setting, choice of music, choice between recorded or live music, volume and quality of sound all need to be considered.

Throughout the ages, philosophers, priests, physicians, scientists, educationalists, psychologists and musicians have observed, and sometimes used the healing power of music. The term "music therapy" has often provoked irrational enthusiasm or unjustified skepticism. Between these extremes lies the fact that music therapy has, within the last 20 years emerged as a rational discipline. Our experience in palliative care suggests that the diversity of its potential is particularly suited to the diversity of the challenges these patients present.

Our special thanks go to Dr. G.C. Meller.

REFERENCES

1. MOUNT BM: The problem of caring for the dying in a general hospital; the palliative care unit as a possible solution. *Can Med Assoc J* 115: 119, 1976
2. SCHULLIAN DM, SCHOEN M (eds): *Music and Medicine, Schumann, New* York, 1948
3. ROEDERER JG: *Introduction to the Physics and Psychophysics of Music,* Springer Verlag, New York, 1973
4. CRITCHLEY M, HENSON RA (eds) *Music and the Brain: Studies in the Neurology of Music,* Heinemann, London, 1977
5. NORDOFF P, ROBBINS CE: *Music Therapy in Special Education,* Magna-music-Baton, St. Louis, MO (in prep.)
6. Idem: *Therapy in Music for Handicapped Children,* St Martin, New York, 1972
7. BONNY HL, PAHNKE WN: The use of music in psychedelic (LSD) psychotherapy. *J Music Ther* 9: 64, 1972
8. BRIGHT R: *Music in Geriatric Care,* St Martin, New York, 1974
9. KORTMAN L: The use of music as a program tool with regressed geriatric patients. *J Gerontol Nurs* 3: 4, 1977
10. SNELL JE: The use of music in group psychotherapy, in *Current Psychiatric Therapies,* vol 5, MASSERMAN JH (ed), Grune, New York, 1965
11. SCHOENBERGER L, BRASWELL C: Music therapy in rehabilitation. *J Rehabil* 37: 30, 1971
12. SPARKS R, HELM N, ALBERT M: Aphasia rehabilitation resulting from melodic intonation therapy. Cortex 10: 303, 1974
13. WASSERMAN NM: Music therapy for the emotionally distrubed in a private hospital. *J Music Ther* 2: 99,1972
14. SAUNDERS C: *The Management of Terminal Illness,* Hosp Med Publ, London, 1967
15. MOUNT BM: *Palliative Care Service* Report, Oct 1976
16. KUBLER-ROSS E: *On Death and Dying,* Macmillan, New York, 1969
17. FRIEDMAN MA: Some practical aids in helping yourself deal with the critically ill patient. Presented at Psychosocial Care of the Dying Patient, San Francisco, June 2-3, 1978
18. ALVIN J: *Music Therapy,* Hutchison, London, 1966
19. GUILHOT MA, GUILHOT J, JOST J, et al: *La Musicotherapie et les Methodes Nouvelles d'Association des Techniques,* Editions ESF, Paris, 1973

LETTERS

MUSIC THERAPY IN PALLIATIVE CARE

CMA Journal, June 9, 1979
Vol. 120

To the editor:

Please reassure me that the article entitled "Music therapy in palliative care" by S. Munro and Dr. B. Mount (Can Med Assoc J 119: 1029, 1978) was meant to be some kind of joke.

Surely we do not need some crackpot therapist with a half-baked degree in psychology to tell us what kind of music to listen to when we are sick. It is well known that "musick hath charms". I can imagine my own chagrin if, under these circumstances, such a therapist told me that perhaps today my psychosocial-spiritual-sexual status precluded my hearing Beethoven's Fifth Symphony and that Mozart's Piano Concerto in C Major would be more suitable.

It is obvious that pleasant music possesses soothing qualities, just as it is obvious that rooms whose walls are garishly striped have an unsettling effect. Therefore, is it necessary to publish such articles in the guise of learned scientific thought when they are merely common sense made muddy and obscure by jargon-ridden balderdash?

David R. Amies, M.D.
10111 Richmond Ave.
Grande Prarie, Alta.

To the editor:

We assure Dr. Amies that no joke was intended in our article. The documented deficiencies in the delivery of health care to terminally ill Canadians are sufficiently serious to render levity, or yet another superficial analysis of the problem, inappropriate. Dr. Amies' letter is an excellent example of Ellis's observation that we react not to facts but to our beliefs about facts.

We concur that it would be unwise to elicit the assistance of a "crackpot therapist with a half-baked degree in psychology". We therefore recommend the use of a therapist who has formal training in music therapy. Such training may be obtained at one Canadian university and at a number of centers in the United States and western Europe. Further information may be obtained from S. Munro, a coauthor of the article, who is currently the president of the Canadian Music Therapy Association.

Dr. Amies need have no concern that if he were terminally ill our music therapist would tell him what music to listen to. Furthermore, we recognize that it is frequently therapeutic to express one's feelings, whether by writing a letter such as his or by listening to Beethoven's Fifth Symphony. I hope that our mandate in administering to a terminally ill Dr. Amies would be to meet him where he is, rather than where we think he should be.

Since Dr. Amies believes the potential therapeutic use of music in a medical setting is "obvious" and "common sense", we are confident that he uses this approach as part of his therapeutic armamentarium. Our article was written for individuals in the medical profession who have had little experience with this approach. Much that is common sense deserves closer scrutiny. Can Dr. Amies be so certain that we have exhausted all benefits that might accrue from a more careful analysis of what is obviously helpful?

As stated in our article, our purpose was not to compile "Learned scientific thought"; we attempted to outline the rationale of using music therapy in palliative care and to offer preliminary observations on the impact of this underused therapeutic tool. In palliative care we are attempting to meet the multidimensional needs of the whole person. We may have to examine areas in health care delivery that have traditionally been neglected if there is to be an improvement.

Dr. Amies' anxiety concerning the use of a music therapist, an approach that apparently falls outside his experience, is understandable. We can only reassure him that the patients appear to have benefited. We thought that our colleagues might be interested in the details of the cases outlined in our article, as they represented some highlights from a fascinating year-long pilot project.

The deficiencies in terminal care in Canada must be recognized as unacceptable. We submit that the individuals responsible must examine new approaches if patient and family suffering is to lessen. Among these approaches music therapy may find a rightful place. As we stated in our article, "the term 'music therapy' has often provoked irrational enthusiasm or unjustified skepticism. Between these extremes lies the fact that music therapy has, within the 20 years, emerged as a rational discipline. Our experience in palliative care suggests that the diversity of its potential is particularly suited to the diversity of the challenges these patients present."

In summary, in so far as Dr. Amies' letter suggests an inordinate tendency towards aggression, anxiety and sarcasm, may we suggest he listen to something soothing - say, Bach's Air on the G-String?

Balfour M. Mount, M.D., F.R.C.S.(C)
Director, Palliative Care Service
Associate Professor of Surgery
McGill University
Montreal, P.O.